101
QUARTERBACK
DRILLS

Steve Axman

ISBN: 1-57167-195-1
Library of Congress Catalog Card Number: 96-69612

Book Design: Mariah Oxford
Cover Design: Joe Buck
Front Cover Photo: Courtesy of the *Dallas Cowboys Weekly*

Coaches Choice Books is a division of: Sagamore Publishing, Inc.
P.O. Box 647
Champaign, IL 61824-0647
Web Site: http//www.sagamorepub.com

DEDICATION

To my partner in life, my wife, Dr. Marie Axman

ACKNOWLEDGMENTS

I acknowledge two great coaches in my belief of using game-like drills as teaching tools. One is Homer Smith, the present offensive coordinator at the University of Arizona and my former head coach at the United States Military Academy at West Point. Homer taught me the importance of specificity of drill practice. The other is Jim McNally, presently the offensive line coach for the Carolina Panthers of the NFL. Jim taught me the importance of the use of drills as teaching and coaching tools.

CONTENTS

The ability of a quarterback to perform on the playing field at a level commensurate with his God-given talent and abilities involves a number of factors—not the least of which is attention to detail. Well-designed drills provide all football players (including quarterbacks) with a constructive means to develop and enhance their essential skills. As such, in order to be appropriately productive, developmental drills should be creative, focused, and time-efficient.

The 101 drills presented in this book represent the best developmental drills for a quarterback that I have seen and used in my 29 years of coaching at the high school, intercollegiate, and professional levels. Each drill offers a terrific tool for teaching a particular attribute of quarterback play. Every drill is designed to be employed by coaches at all competitive levels.

To the extent that *101 Quarterback Drills* helps you maximize the inherent abilities of your players and improve the on-the-field performance of your team, then the time and effort necessary to write this book will have been well worthwhile.

CHAPTER 1

PASSING DRILLS

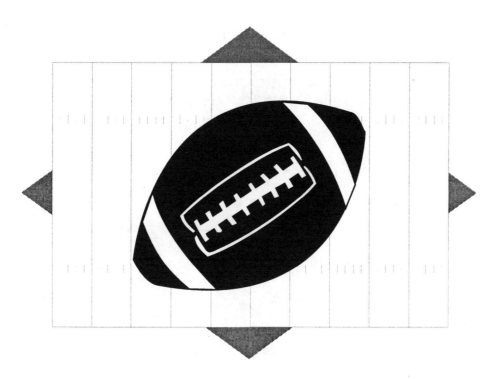

DRILL #1: WARM UP THROW DRILL

Objective: To warm up all body parts for the actual passing/throwing motion, especially the passing arm.

Equipment Needed: One football; lined field.

Description: Two quarterbacks stand 10 yards apart working on a yard line. The passer stands on the balls of both feet. He checks for proper body stance: knees bent, football held up high near the throwing shoulder, back elbow up away from the body frame. The quarterback takes a proper pass delivery step just outside of the yard line and executes a proper pass delivery action of the football.

Coaching Points:

- The coach should check for proper carriage of the body and pre-pass delivery stance.

- The quarterback steps beyond the yard line to properly open the hips for fluid pass delivery action.

- The coach should emphasize bisecting the opposite quarterback, focusing on proper pass delivery stepping and follow-through action of the body.

- As his arm warms up, the passing quarterback attempts to get horizontal accuracy by trying to hit the quarterback being thrown to "in the nose."

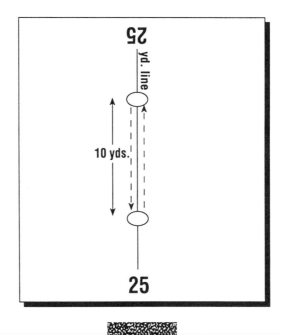

DRILL #2: QUARTERBACK-RECEIVER
WARM UP THROW DRILL

Objective: To warm up all body parts for the actual passing/throwing motion, especially the passing arm.

Equipment Needed: One football per two quarterbacks; lined field.

Description: A quarterback stands 10 yards from a receiver working on a yard line. The passer stands on the balls of both feet. He checks for proper body stance: knees bent, football held up high near the throwing shoulder, back elbow up away from the body frame. The quarterback takes a proper pass delivery step just outside of the yard line and executes a proper pass delivery action of the football to the receiver. The receiver gently tosses the football underhand to the quarterback next to him so that quarterback can execute the same practice action.

Coaching Points:

- The coach should check for proper carriage of the body and pre-pass delivery stance.

- The quarterback steps beyond the yard line to properly open the hips for fluid pass delivery action.

- The coach should emphasize bisecting the opposite receiver, focusing on proper pass delivery stepping and a follow-through action of the body.

- As his arm warms up, the passing quarterback attempts to get horizontal accuracy by trying to hit the receiver being thrown to "in the nose."

- This drill is good for pre-game warm up so a quarterback doesn't jam his fingers.

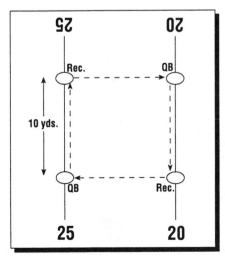

DRILL #3: WRIST WARM UP THROW DRILL

Objective: To warm up the wrist of the passing hand.

Equipment Needed: One football; lined field.

Description: Two quarterbacks stand approximately seven yards apart from one another facing each other. With a normal pre-pass high hold of the football (above the throwing shoulder), the passing quarterback executes normal high, over the top of the ear pass delivery. However, at the highest point of the pass delivery, rather than a natural follow-through action of passing arm, the quarterback unnaturally breaks his wrist to "flick" the football to the opposite quarterback.

Coaching Points:

- This drill is an artificial one since we would never want the quarterback to break his wrist during the pass delivery action. It is meant to warm up the wrist only.

- The delivery of the pass is made with a snapping break of the wrist.

- The passing quarterback should attempt index finger follow-through to the opposite quarterback's nose.

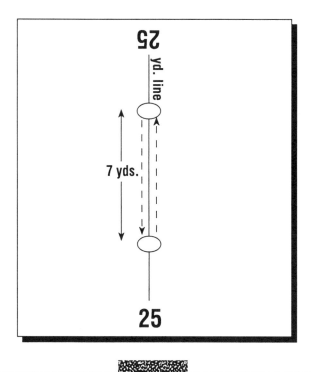

DRILL #4: HIP WARM UP THROW DRILL

Objective: To warm up and loosen the hips for the pass delivery motion.

Equipment Needed: One football; lined field.

Description: Two quarterbacks stand eight to ten yards apart working on a yard line. The passers stand on the line with the balls of the feet both starting out with a 90° angle turn to the right. Without moving the feet the quarterbacks open their upper torso to the left and execute a proper over-the-top delivery motion to the nose of the other quarterback. After sufficient repetitions, the action is repeated with the feet turned on a 90° angle to the left.

Coaching Points:

- No stepping action is involved in this drill. The feet face away from the line on a 90° angle to the left and right.

- The quarterback must be sure to raise the football above the shoulder in the pre-throw stance to execute a proper "over-the-top" pass delivery.

- Since no stepping action is involved, extra index finger follow-through to the opposite quarterback's nose should be emphasized.

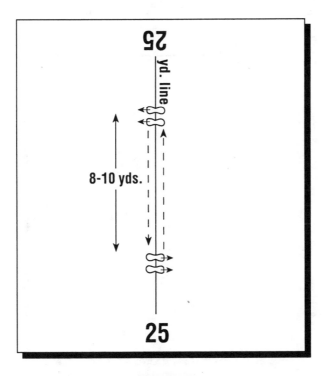

DRILL #5: VARYING FOOT POSITION DRILL

Objective: To develop proper upper body throwing action while separating such action from the lower body set-up or move run platform.

Equipment Needed: One football per two quarterbacks.

Description: Two quarterbacks face one another at a distance of eight to ten yards. Passes are executed by placing the feet at varying angles away from a direct facing of the opposite quarterback. The quarterbacks practice throwing with their feet on a 45° angle, a 90° angle and a 135° angle, both to the left and right as the upper body is turned to the opposite quarterback.

Coaching Points:

- At each angle positioning, the quarterback must be sure to raise his level shoulder throwing platform with a high, near the back shoulder hold of the football.

- Since the quarterback cannot step at the target point, extra index finger follow-through should be emphasized.

- At the 135° angle, the trunk twist will be overly contorted. However, it will help the quarterback to practice the upper body throwing action at its most extreme divorce from the lower body leg action.

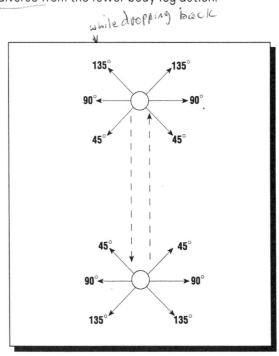

DRILL #6: KNEELING THROW DRILL

Objective: To warm up the upper body torso, shoulders and passing arm.

Equipment Needed: One football; lined field.

Description: Two quarterbacks kneel with their left knee up (left foot just outside the line to ensure proper open hip action), seven to eight yards apart. The quarterbacks execute proper over-the-top pass delivery action with proper index finger follow-through to the opposite quarterback's nose. After a sufficient number of repetitions, the quarterbacks switch to a double knee kneel action and then to the right knee up.

Coaching Points:

- Through all three kneeling actions (left knee up, both knees down, right knee up), the passing quarterback must emphasize a proper high pre-pass hold of the football near the throwing shoulder.

- The variation of the knee positioning helps to vary the hold of the upper body torso during the various pass deliveries.

- Driving the ball with the chest should be emphasized.

- When both knees are down, the quarterback actually falls to the ground as he rolls into the throw with his belly and chest. The quarterbacks do not snap and break at the hips during this pass delivery action.

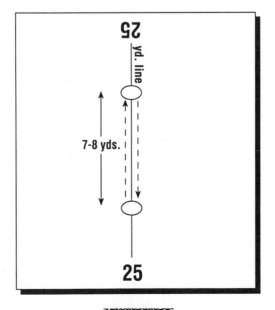

DRILL #7: PRANCER THROW DRILL

Objective: To emphasize the "feel" of rolling the body over the ball of the front pass delivery step.

Equipment Needed: One football; lined field.

Description: Two quarterbacks stand eight to ten yards apart on a yard line. The passer stands over the line with his forward pass delivery step foot just beyond the line (to help properly open the hips for the pass delivery). The front leg is bent. The heel of the front foot is off the ground to help form the "prancer" stance. The quarterback executes his normal "over-the-top" pass delivery action, emphasizing driving the ball with the chest and the rolling over the ball of the front foot.

Coaching Points:

- The quarterback should roll his body (especially his chest) over the ball of the front, pass delivery step foot.

- The quarterback should be sure to execute a proper high hold of the football near the passing shoulder as he begins the rollover pass delivery action.

- Proper index finger follow-through should be emphasized.

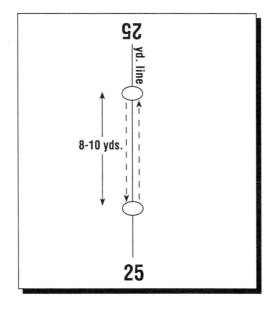

DRILL #8: OFF BALANCE THROW DRILL

Objective: To practice the skills of proper pass delivery when not set properly due to pass rush.

Equipment Needed: One football per two quarterbacks.

Description: The quarterback is instructed, from a pre-snap stance with football in hand, to deliver a pass to the opposite quarterback off of the second or third step to the left and then to the right. The quarterbacks align seven to eight yards from one another.

Coaching Points:

- The quarterback should move away from his pre-snap stance as if under the center to the left or right and throw quickly from an unbalanced position off his second or third step.

- The quarterback, in an almost jump pass-type action, should get the football up into a high, near the throwing shoulder hold and execute a pass delivery with extra index finger follow-through.

- The extra index finger follow-through and raised upper body torso separated from the off-balance lower run platform are critical.

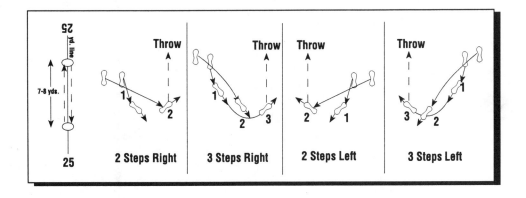

DRILL #9: ACCURACY DRILL

Objective: To practice passing accuracy in a competitive, fun setting.

Equipment Needed: One football per two quarterbacks; lined field.

Description: Two quarterbacks stand ten yards apart and throw passes to one another from a proper pre-pass set-up stance. They score each other for accuracy. If the pass were to hit the opposite quarterback in the face—3 points, within one foot outside the face—2 points, one to three feet from the face—1 point. After six or seven repetitions, the quarterbacks can expand to 15 yards, 20 yards, 25 yards, etc. The first to 50 points wins.

Coaching Points:

- The coach should check for proper pre-pass delivery stance on each repetition.

- The coach should check for proper stepping action, drive of the football with the chest and index finger follow-through to the pass delivery (the face) target.

- Special emphasis should be placed on the index finger follow-through: Where was the finger pointing when the ball was released?

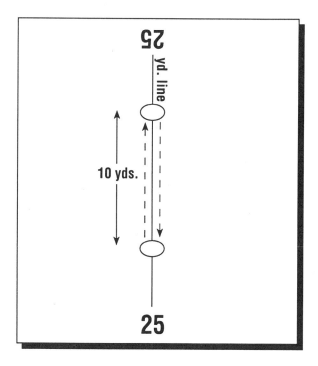

DRILL #10: TARGET PASS DRILL

Objective: To develop pure passing accuracy.

Equipment Needed: Six to eight footballs; passing target net.

Description: Off of the various drops used in one's specific offense, the quarterbacks throw at the target(s) on a passing net. Left hash, right hash and middle of the field considerations should be taken into account.

Coaching Points:

- The coach should look for proper lead foot stepping, drive of the football with the chest and index finger follow-through at the target point. All of these body parts must be in a direct line to the target spot.

- The quarterback can start at a depth of 10 yards and gradually work backwards to whatever depth the coach feels the quarterback can handle in relation to arm strength.

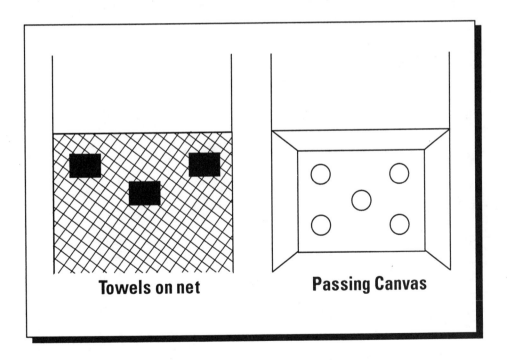

Towels on net   **Passing Canvas**

DRILL #11: SWINGING TIRE TARGET DRILL

Objective: To develop passing accuracy to a moving target.

Equipment Needed: Six to eight footballs; moving tire target.

Description: Off of the various drops used in one's specific offense, the quarterbacks throw at a moving tire target suspended from a goalpost. Left hash, right hash and middle of the field considerations should be taken into account.

Coaching Points:

- The coach should look for proper lead foot stepping, drive of the football with the chest and index finger follow-through at the moving target point. All of these body parts must be directed in a straight line to the moving target spot.

- The quarterback should throw to where the tire is moving to, not at the tire.

- The quarterback can start at a depth of 10 yards and gradually work backwards to whatever depth the coach feels the quarterback can handle in relation to arm strength.

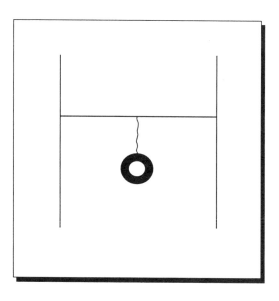

DRILL #12: TRAJECTORY PASS DRILL

Objective: To practice the different type of trajectories (straight line, intermediate and high) that are needed for varying types of passes.

Equipment Needed: One football per two quarterbacks.

Description: Two quarterbacks start out 20 yards apart from one another. Six passes are thrown. Two are low drill passes. Two have intermediate trajectory. Two have high trajectory. After the six passes, the quarterbacks back up five yards and repeat the set of six passes. Depending on arm strength, the quarterbacks can continue to a distance of 40 or 50 yards.

Coaching Points:

- This drill helps the quarterbacks understand the different types of trajectory that they need to put on various passes.

- The quarterbacks should follow through to the zenith (highest) point of the pass with their lead step, chest and index finger follow-through.

- Proper follow-through to the zenith point of the pass allows the football to turn over and drop in to the receiver (target) nose down. Lack of follow-through to the zenith point of the pass will lead to a nose-up football which "dies" due to the fat of the football cutting through the air.

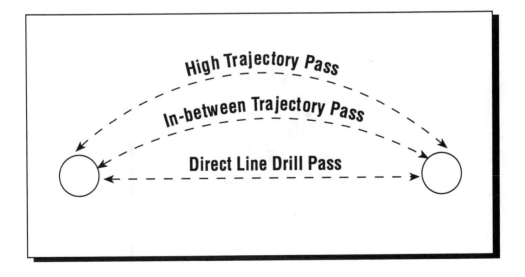

DRILL #13: TRAJECTORY NET PASS DRILL

Objective: To teach and practice high trajectory passes with the nose of the football turning over so that the football drops in nose-down.

Equipment Needed: 10-12 footballs; portable passing target net; lined field.

Description: Starting from an alignment twenty yards from a portable passing target net, the quarterbacks take their normal three-, five-, or seven-step drop (or whatever other drop action is used) and execute a high trajectory pass that drops nose-down into the passing target net. Left hash, right hash and middle of the field adjustments should be considered. After a desired number of passes from each hash and the middle of the field, the passing net is moved back five yards. The quarterbacks should practice such deep trajectory passes to both the left and the right.

Coaching Points:

- The quarterback should follow through to the zenith (highest) point of the pass with their lead step, chest and index finger follow-through.

- Proper follow-through to the zenith point of the pass allows the football to turn over and drop in to the receiver (target) nose down. Lack of follow-through to the zenith point of the pass will lead to a nose-up football which "dies" due to the fat of the football cutting through the air.

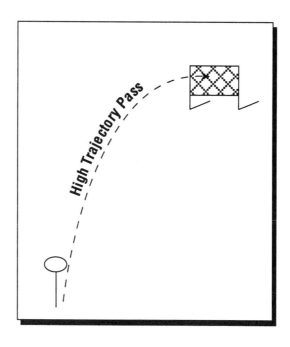

DRILL #14: 2 DEEP HOLE THROW NET DRILL

Objective: To teach and practice throwing a straight line, drill-type pass into the 2 Deep fade hole between a squatted cornerback and a 2 Deep hash safety.

Equipment Needed: Six to eight footballs; two stand-up dummies; lined field; passing target net.

Description: From the normal drops he takes in his specific offense, the quarterback practices the 2 Deep fade hole throw on the sideline at a distance of 18-22 yards into a passing target net. Two stand-up dummies can be set up to simulate a squatted 2 Deep cornerback and a 2 Deep hash safety, or managers or scout squad personnel can be utilized to help simulate the deep zone coverage. Left hash, right hash, and middle of the field alignment considerations should be taken into account.

Coaching Points:

- The coach can add a potential dump route to the drill and have the cornerback drop off instead of squatting or have the safety roll off the hash to simulate taking away the fade hole throw.

- This pass is a drill-the-football-into-the-hole throw to eliminate the possibility of the 2 Deep personnel getting to the pass.

- Wide receivers can be used to run the 2 Deep Fade adjust routes in place of the passing target net.

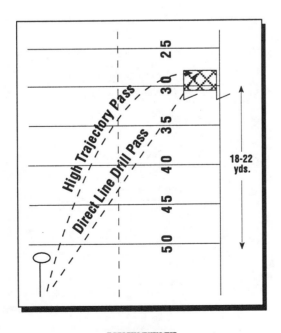

DRILL #15: HASH HOLE THROW NET DRILL

Objective: To practice throwing a pass to a vertical receiver working up the hash.

Equipment Needed: Six to eight footballs; lined field.

Description: Off the various drops used in his specific offense, the quarterback throws either a flat line drill pass or a touch, drop-in pass over linebackers to a distance of 18-22 yards upfield. Left hash, right hash and middle of the field considerations should be taken into account.

Coaching Points:

• If the receiver is wide open (linebackers not in the way), the football is drilled in with a flat, low trajectory pass.

• If the linebackers are dropping in the path of the throw (must be simulated by the coach, a manager or a scout team linebacker), the quarterback must produce a touch pass and drop it in over the head of the linebackers.

• The quarterback should not lob the pass over the head of a linebacker in fear of setting up a big hit by a safety.

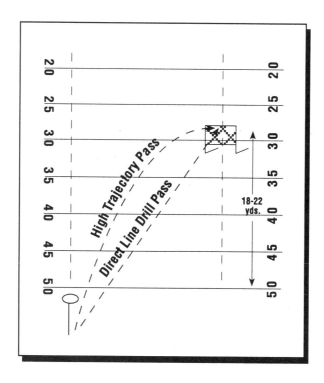

DRILL #16: GOAL LINE FADE NET PASS DRILL

Objective: To teach and practice the quick fade pass in the goal line or Red Zone area off quick two-, three- or five-step drops.

Equipment Needed: Six to eight footballs; lined goal line/Red Zone area.

Description: This drill is executed in the same fashion as the Trajectory Net Pass Drill with the exception that the passing target net is set in a fixed position one yard by one yard inside the backline corner end zone flag. The quarterbacks start from a position on the one yard line and work back to the fifteen yard line practicing high trajectory Fade route throws in which the football drops nose down into the passing target net. Passes from the one to the five yard line necessitate a quick two-step drop. From the five yard to about the 15, a three-step drop is taken. From the 15 yard line out, a quick five-step drop is utilized. Left hash, right hash, and middle of the field considerations are taken into account. The quarterback should also practice throwing to both the left and right.

Coaching Points:

- The quarterbacks should follow-through to the zenith (highest) point of the pass with their lead step, chest and index finger follow-through.

- Proper follow-through to the zenith point of the pass allows for the football to turn over and drop in to the receiver (target) nose down. Lack of follow-through to the zenith point of the pass will lead to a nose-up football which "dies" due to the fat of the football cutting through the air.

- The coach should help develop the proper sense of the quick timing or release needed in this shortened area of the field off of two-, three-, and quick five-step drops.

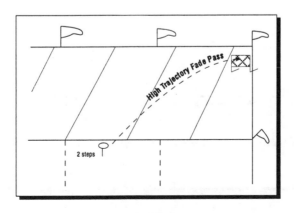

DRILL #17: DOWN THE LINE MOVE PASS DRILL

Objective: To practice on-the-move passing.

Equipment Needed: One football per two quarterbacks; lined field.

Description: Two quarterbacks start on the sideline, each on a yard line 10 yards apart. The quarterback with the football jogs in place until the other quarterback runs out in front of him approximately five yards. At that point, the quarterback with the football runs forward and executes a pass on the run. When the opposite quarterback catches the pass he jogs in place until the other quarterback runs to a position five yards in front. That quarterback then begins running and executes an on-the-move pass. The repetitions are repeated all across the field.

Coaching Points:

- The coach should emphasize a high, near-the-shoulder carriage of the football, divorcing the upper-body passing action from the lower-body run action.

- Extra index finger follow-through should be emphasized to help fight the negative influence of the lower-body run action.

- The passing quarterback attempts to lead the other quarterback by a yard.

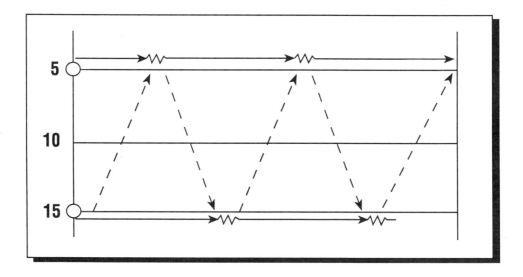

DRILL #18: CIRCLE PASSING DRILL

Objective: To develop proper passing-on-the-move skills. To teach quarterbacks to separate their upper-body throwing platform from their lower-body running platform in their move passing action.

Equipment Needed: One football per two quarterbacks; a circle with a 10-yard diameter drawn in chalk on the practice field.

Description: Two quarterbacks, 180° apart from one another, run the circle in a clockwise direction and execute their move passing techniques back and forth throwing to both the left and right. After a designated time period, the quarterbacks run in a counter-clockwise direction and repeat the drill.

Coaching Points:

- The coach may set up three circles with 10, 12 1/2, and 15 yard diameters so quarterbacks can practice their move throwing at such distances.

- At 12 1/2 and 15 yard distances, three quarterbacks can go at the same time.

- A raised, level throwing platform (high hold of the football near the back throwing shoulder) is essential.

- This drill actually overemphasizes separating of the upper-throwing platform and the lower-running platform because the passer is throwing behind his body position as he works around the circle. Leading with the chest and extra index finger follow-through are paramount to a good move pass delivery.

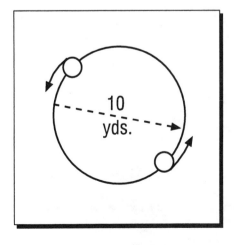

DRILL #19: QUICK RELEASE PASS DRILL

Objective: To develop the skill of a quick passing release from a set position.

Equipment Needed: One football per quarterback.

Description: Two receivers are positioned 12 yards from the quarterback and seven yards apart. A defender splits the two at a depth of eight to nine yards. From a straight drop-back and setup position, the quarterback waits for the defender to make an initial break declaration to cover one receiver or the other. Once the defender has made such an initial break, the quarterback attempts to drill the other receiver with a quick release pass before the defender can readjust to the flight of the ball to intercept it or knock it down. The only rule the defender must follow is to take two steps toward the initial receiver before he reacts to the football.

Coaching Points:

- The quarterback should be fully cocked (shoulder and arm of throwing arm) so there is absolutely no delay in the delivery. The football should be held high and off the back breast.

- The quarterback should be sure to combine the quick release action with proper index finger follow-through.

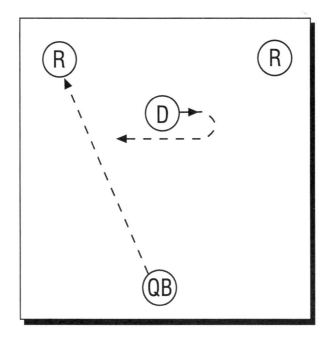

DRILL #20: OPEN MAN PASS DRILL

Objective: To help the quarterback to develop his peripheral vision to find the open receiver, adjust his body set-up position to the open receiver, and get off a quick release pass with accuracy.

Equipment Needed: One football per quarterback.

Description: Four or five receivers are placed randomly in the field, bending over with their hands on their knees. Without the quarterback knowing, the coach designates one receiver to pop up quickly once the quarterback has set up. The quarterback executes one of his normal drop-back actions, sets up, locates the open receiver, adjusts his set if necessary and throws a quick release pass to the popped-up receiver.

Coaching Points:

- The receiver who is to pop up signifying the open receiver should wait until the quarterback has set up off his dropback action. This gives the quarterback the opportunity to reset so he can practice his foot and body position readjustment action.

- The quarterback should not allow the readjustment set-up stepping action to disturb his proper stepping and follow-through action of his passing mechanics.

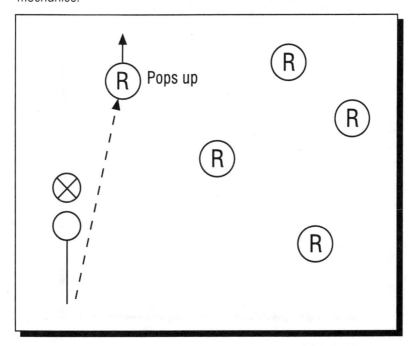

DRILL #21: OPEN MAN BREAKOUT PASS DRILL

Objective: To develop the quarterback's ability to find the open receiver; to practice delivering an accurate, quick release pass.

Equipment Needed: One football per quarterback.

Description: The quarterback executes one of his normal pass drop actions. On a signal by the coach, three randomly placed receivers, all tightly covered by pass defenders, break out in whatever fashion they wish from their man-to-man coverage and get open to receive a pass. The receivers act much as they would if they were in a touch football game in their efforts to get open and receive a pass. The quarterback must locate an open, or the most open, receiver and drill him with a quickly released, accurate pass.

Coaching Points:

- The coach should emphasize the quick release action once the quarterback has located an open receiver.

- The quarterback should throw the pass as the receiver begins to break open. If he waits for the receiver to become open, he may be too late, for the defender will be given time to readjust to the receiver, interfere with the pass or make an interception.

- The quarterback should lead the receiver away from the man coverage once the receiver has separated from the defender.

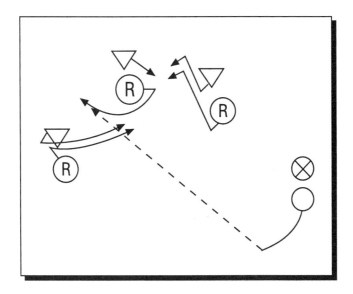

DRILL #22: ROCK-DROP DRILL

Objective: To practice the proper rocking action of the football across the belly as the quarterback drops back to set up.

Equipment Needed: One football per quarterback; lined field.

Description: A line of quarterbacks faces down a yard line stripe. One quarterback toes the sideline. On the coach's cadence, the quarterback practices his rocking drop-back action down the yard line stripe to the nearest hash. Each quarterback goes until the line is finished. The quarterbacks repeat, coming back.

Coaching Points:

- The coach should check for a proper 30° body tilt from perpendicular in the dropping back for depth action and make sure the quarterback drops his back.

- The quarterback should not prance (body perpendicular to ground with knees going straight up and down). This action shortens the actual drop.

- The coach should check for a proper rock of the football across the belly area to aid smooth dropping, as well as smooth stepping down the yard line strip.

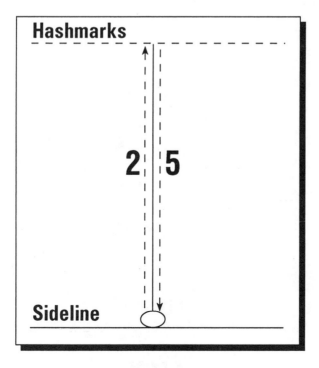

DRILL #23: SET-UP DRILL

Objective: To practice the drop-back set-up actions that a particular offense may utilize.

Equipment Needed: One football per quarterback; lined field.

Description: Quarterbacks form a horizontal line along a yard line (to measure depth of drop). They take a pre-snap alignment, holding a football as if they were positioned to take a snap from the center. On one quarterback's cadence, they will all take the same, designated three-step, five-step, seven-step move, etc. drop-back action to the desired set-up launch point.

Coaching Points:

- The coach should check for proper depth and proper set-up action.

- It is important for the quarterback to have a proper, athletic carriage of the body in his pre-pass stance.

- On each repetition, the coach should tell the quarterbacks what set-up angle he wants (passing to the left/center/right) so the quarterbacks can practice such set-up actions.

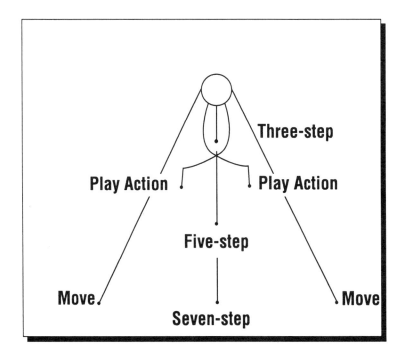

DRILL #24: RE-SET DRILL

Objective: To practice re-set actions after the prime set-up to ensure athletic carriage of the body in the passing stance on a second, third, and fourth, possibly, re-set; to develop re-set athleticism and quick-footedness.

Equipment Needed: One football; lined field.

Description: Two quarterbacks align facing one another five yards apart. They toe the yard line to measure the depth of the drop. The coach stands in between the two quarterbacks. The quarterback with the football takes a three-, five-, or seven-step drop and sets up in a proper pre-pass delivery stance. The coach then uses hand signals to either bail out set-up left or right, shuffle a yard or two left or right, act as if he's ducking under a jumping defensive lineman or step up into the pocket. The coach signals for three such re-sets. On the third re-set, the quarterback throws to the opposite quarterback. The exercise is then repeated by the other quarterback.

Coaching Points:

- Re-sets due to rush pressure are where quarterbacks often break down in their passing mechanics by resetting into improper pre-pass delivery stances.

- The coach should check each re-set stance for proper knee bend, athletic carriage of the body and a high hold of the football in the vicinity of the back, throwing shoulder. The quarterback should not lock out his legs or hold the football at belt level.

- A right-handed quarterback bailing out to his left should bail-out with his back to the LOS to try to run over-the-top of a backside defensive end rush that he might not see.

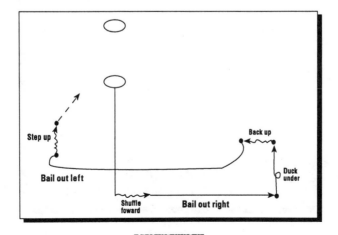

DRILL #25: STRAIGHT DROP BACK SET-UP AND THROW DRILL

Objective: To tie together the drop-back set-up skills of the Set-Up Drill and the plant-throw action skills of the straight drop-back action.

Equipment Needed: One football per two quarterbacks; lined field.

Description: This drill is the next step in the teaching progression of the coordinated pass drop and pass delivery for straight drop-back pass action. Two quarterbacks face one another, five to ten yards apart. On cadence, the quarterback with the football takes the determined drop (three-, five-, seven- step). He delivers a pass to the opposite quarterback and then comes back to his original alignment. The other quarterback executes the drill in the same fashion.

Coaching Points:

- The quarterbacks should be told by the coach what type of pass delivery to execute.

- The coach should check for the integration of the straight drop-back set-up skills and straight drop-back pass-delivery skills.

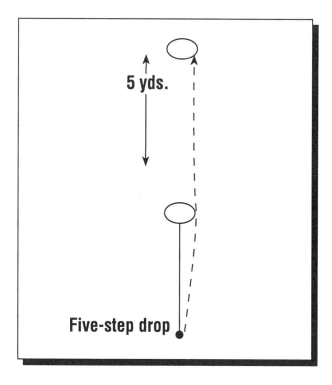

DRILL #26: SET-UP AND THROW LEFT DRILL

Objective: To teach, coach and practice the specialized skills of a right-handed quarterback throwing to his left.

Equipment Needed: One football per two quarterbacks; lined field.

Description: Two quarterbacks align on two yard lines, 15 yards in front of one another and 15 yards in width. The quarterbacks take turns dropping back taking a left sideline pass delivery set attitude and delivering a pass to the left.

Coaching Points:

- This drill is simply reversed for a left-handed quarterback throwing to his right.

- The initial key is for the quarterback to properly take a cheat step with his back right plant foot step to cheat set his hips to the left. This step enables the quarterback to now deliver a straight-line pass to left eliminating the over-swing of the body to the left.

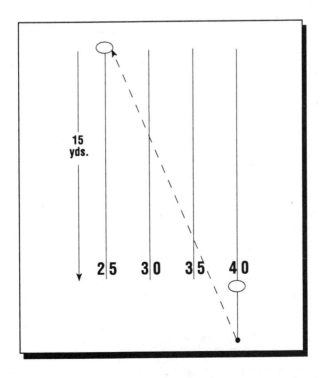

DRILL #27: MOVE PASS SET-UP AND THROW DRILL

Objective: To tie together the move launch point (usually on the inside leg or over the tackle) drop-back set-up skills of the Set-Up Drill and the pass-action skills of the move pass delivery.

Equipment Needed: One football per two quarterbacks; lined field.

Description: This drill is the next step in the teaching progression of the coordinated pass drop and pass delivery for the move drop back-pass action. Two quarterbacks align on the opposite hashes 5 to 10 yards in front of each other. On cadence, the quarterback with the football executes a proper move pass-drop set-up. He delivers a pass to the opposite quarterback off the move set-up launch point, then returns to his original alignment so that the other quarterback then executes the drill.

Coaching Points:

- The quarterback should be told by the coach what type of pass delivery to execute.

- The coach should check for the integration of the move set-up skills and pass-delivery skills.

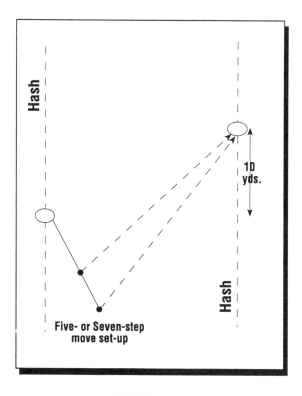

DRILL #28: PLAY ACTION PASS SET-UP AND THROW DRILL

Objective: To tie together the play action pass set-up skills of the play action passes used by a particular offense and the pass-action skills of the play action pass deliveries.

Equipment Needed: One football per two quarterbacks; lined field.

Description: This drill is the next step in the teaching progression of the coordinated pass drop and pass delivery for the play action passes for the particular play action passes of an offense. Two quarterbacks face one another, 5 to 10 yards apart. On cadence, the quarterback with the football executes the desired play action pass set-up from the quarterback's particular offense. He delivers a play action pass to the opposite quarterback and then comes back to his original alignment. The other quarterback then executes the drill.

Coaching Points:

- The quarterback should be told by the coach what type of play action pass delivery to execute, in regard to set-up and timing of throw (five-step, seven-step, plant/throw, pop-up/throw, hitch-up/throw, etc.).

- The coach should check for the integration of the play action drop-back action skills and the play action pass-delivery skills.

- After the run fake action, emphasis should be placed on getting the football up to have a high pre-pass carriage of the football.

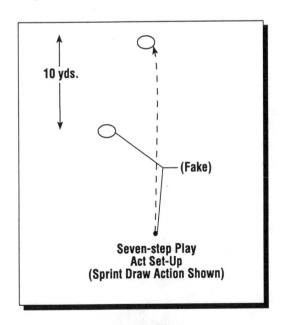

10 yds.

(Fake)

**Seven-step Play
Act Set-Up
(Sprint Draw Action Shown)**

DRILL #29: BOOTLEG/WAGGLE PASS THROW DRILL

Objective: To tie together the bootleg/waggle pass set-up skills of the Set-Up Drill and the pass action skills of the bootleg/waggle pass delivery.

Equipment Needed: One football per two quarterbacks; lined field.

Description: This drill is the next step in the teaching progression of the coordinated pass drop and pass delivery of the bootleg/waggle pass action. Two quarterbacks align on the opposite hashes 10 yards in front of each other. On cadence, the quarterback with the football executes a proper bootleg/waggle pass drop set up. He delivers a pass to the opposite quarterback off the bootleg/waggle set-up launch point and returns to his original alignment. The other quarterback then executes the drill.

Coaching Points:

- Many teams utilize bootleg/waggle passing to throw on the run rather than as set-up action. In this case, the coach should follow the thoughts of the Sprint-Out/Roll-Out and Throw Drill.

- After the run fake and bootleg/waggle stem action to the pass delivery launch point, the coach should check for a good pre-pass delivery set-up with a high carriage of the football.

- The quarterback should be told by the coach what type of pass delivery to execute (plant/throw, pop-up/throw, hitch-up throw).

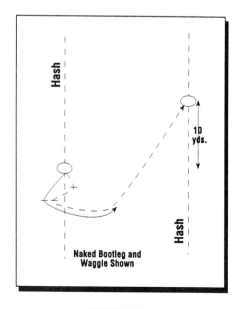

Naked Bootleg and Waggle Shown

Hash · 10 yds. · Hash · Naked Bootleg and Waggle Shown

Naked Bootleg and Waggle Shown

DRILL #30: SPRINT-OUT/ROLL-OUT AND THROW DRILL

Objective: To tie together the sprint-out/roll-out perimeter attack run action skills and the pass action skills of sprint-out/roll-out action pass delivery action.

Equipment Needed: One football per two quarterbacks; lined field.

Description: This drill is the next step in the teaching progression of the coordinated sprint-out/roll-out run action and pass delivery. Two quarterbacks align on the opposite hashes 10 yards in front of each other. On cadence, the quarterback with the football executes a proper sprint-out/roll-out pass drop action. He delivers a sprint-out/roll-out pass on the run to the opposite quarterback, and runs back to his original alignment so that the other quarterback can execute the drill.

Coaching Points:

- The coach should see that the quarterback steps up to the pass target point after he gets to the highest point of the sprint-out/roll-out action.

- For proper throwing on the run action, the quarterback should get the football back up so that the throw can be released over-the-top.

- Since the lower-body run action wants to detract from the upper-body throw action, the quarterback needs to emphasize extra index finger follow-through to the target point of the pass.

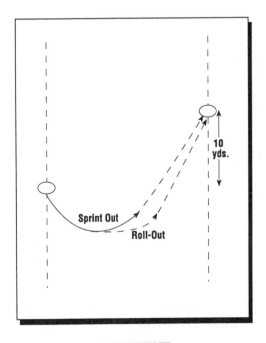

DRILL #31: INDIVIDUAL BACKFIELD PASS ROUTE DRILL

Objective: To practice the individual backfield pass route throws.

Equipment Needed: Eight to ten footballs; line spacing tapes or hoses.

Description: Off of three-, five-, or seven-step timed drops (or any other drop-back move, roll-out, sprint-out or play action), two quarterbacks practice passing to individual backfield pass routes at the same time. A manager should help assist in the return of the footballs so that as many passes can be thrown as possible in the allotted time period. Throws should be made equally to the left and right. Left hash, right hash and middle of the field considerations should be taken into account.

Coaching Points:

- Since back routes are often short control routes, the quarterbacks should not relax in their pre-pass delivery stances. It is a natural tendency for quarterbacks to lock their legs out and become flat-footed on short back-route passes.

- If the back-route passes are short, control-type passes, the quarterbacks should use extra index finger follow-through, since they do not have to drive the thrown football with their chests.

- Conversely, on all-out or flat-pass throws, the quarterback should be sure to drive the pass with his chest to provide proper body torque power.

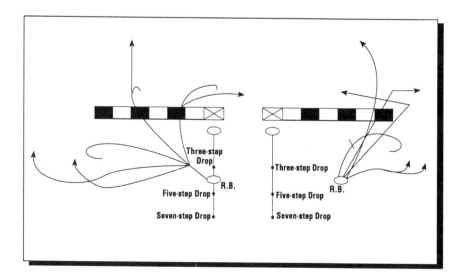

DRILL #32: INDIVIDUAL TIGHT END PASS-ROUTE DRILL

Objective: To practice the individual tight end pass-route throws.

Equipment Needed: Eight to ten footballs; line spacing tapes or hoses.

Description: Off of three-, five-, or seven-step timed drops (or any other drop-back move, roll-out, sprint-out or play action), two quarterbacks practice passing to individual tight end pass routes at the same time. A manager should help assist in the return of the footballs so that as many passes can be thrown as possible in the allotted time period. Throws should be made equally to the left and right. Left hash, right hash and middle of the field considerations should be made.

Coaching Points:

- As in the Individual Backfield Pass-Route Drill, many of the tight end routes can be short control routes. In this case, the quarterbacks should not relax in their pre-pass delivery stances. It is a natural tendency for quarterbacks to lock their legs out and become flat-footed on short tight end route passes.

- If the back-route passes are short, control-type passes, the quarterbacks should use extra index finger follow-through since they do not have to drive the thrown football with their chests.

- The coach should be sure the quarterback is properly warmed up before any deep throwing is practiced.

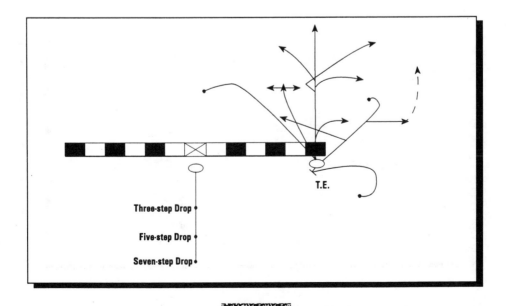

DRILL #33: INDIVIDUAL WIDE RECEIVER PASS-ROUTE DRILL

Objective: To practice the individual wide receiver pass route throws.

Equipment Needed: 10-12 footballs; line spacing tapes or hoses.

Description: Off of three-, five-, or seven-step timed drops (or any other drop back, move, roll-out, sprint-out or play action), two quarterbacks practice passing to individual wide receiver pass routes at the same time. A manager should help assist in the return of the footballs so that as many passes can be thrown as possible in the allotted time period. Throws should be made equally to the left and right. Left hash, right hash and middle of the field considerations should be made.

Coaching Points:

- The coach should be sure to progress from shorter routes to deeper routes to be sure that the quarterback's arm is properly warmed up.

- As in the Individual Backfield and Tight End Individual Route Drills, the coach should be sure to vary the drop back, sprint-out, roll-out, move-out, and play action of the coach's particular offense.

- In the Individual Backfield, Tight End and Wide Receiver Route Drills, the coach should allot extra repetitions to the more difficult routes and/or throws.

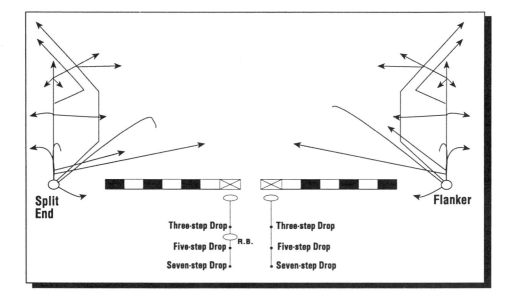

DRILL #34: INDIVIDUAL SHORT PASS-ROUTE DRILL

Objective: To practice the individual short pass-route throws of all positions.

Equipment Needed: 12 footballs; two spacing tapes or hoses.

Description: Off of three-, five-, or seven-step timed drops (or any other drop back, move, sprint-out, roll-out or play action), two quarterbacks practice their individual short pass-route passing to all receiving positions at the same time. A manager should help assist in the return of the footballs so that as many passes can be thrown as possible in the allotted time period. Throws should be made equally to the left and right. Left hash, right hash and middle of the field considerations should be made.

Coaching Points:

- On any short control routes, the quarterbacks should be sure not to relax in their pre-pass delivery stances. It is a natural tendency for quarterbacks to lock their legs out and become flat-footed on such short passes.

- If the routes are short, control passes, the quarterback should use extra index finger follow-through since he may not have to drive the thrown football with his chest (still necessitating proper follow through).

- Conversely, on all-out or flat-pass throws, the quarterback should be sure to drive the pass with his chest to provide proper body torque power.

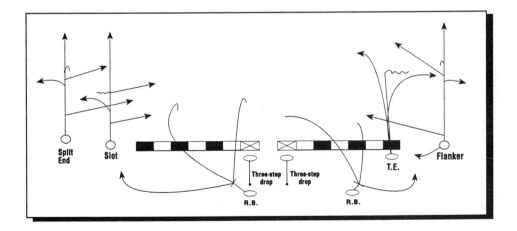

DRILL #35: INDIVIDUAL INTERMEDIATE PASS ROUTE DRILL

Objective: To practice individual intermediate pass route throws of all positions.

Equipment Needed: 12 footballs; two line-spacing tapes or hoses.

Description: Off of three-, five-, or seven-step timed drops (or any other drop back, move, sprint-out, roll-out or play action), two quarterbacks practice their individual intermediate pass route passing to all receiving positions at the same time. A manager should help assist in the return of the footballs so that as may passes can be thrown as possible in the allotted time period. Throws should be made equally to the left and right. Left hash, right hash and middle of the field considerations should be made.

Coaching Points:

- The coach should be sure to check for the proper pass timing for each particular intermediate route throw (plant throw or plant pop-up and throw) for the (normal) five-step intermediate route throw timing.

- On all-out or flat-type throws, the quarterback should be sure to drive the pass with his chest to provide proper body torque power.

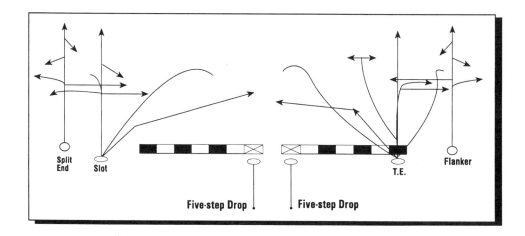

DRILL #36: INDIVIDUAL DEEP PASS ROUTE DRILL

Objective: To practice individual deep pass route throws for all positions.

Equipment Needed: 12 footballs; two line spacing tapes or hoses.

Description: Off of three-, five-, or seven-step timed drops (or any other drop back, move, sprint-out, roll-out or play action), two quarterbacks practice their individual deep pass route passing to all receiving positions at the same time. A manager should help assist in the return of the footballs so that as many passes can be thrown as possible in the allotted time period. Throws should be made equally to the left and right. Left hash, right hash and middle of the field considerations should be made.

Coaching Points:

- On all deep throws, the coach should check for proper pass timing for each particular deep route (three-step plant throw, five- or seven-step pop-up or hitch-up throws, etc.).

- The quarterback should drive the ball with his chest on all deep throws to provide proper body torque power.

- On deep streaks, post-corners and over-the-top posts, the quarterback should be sure to follow through to the zenith (highest) point of the pass to get the football to properly turn over, nose down, as it descends to the receiver.

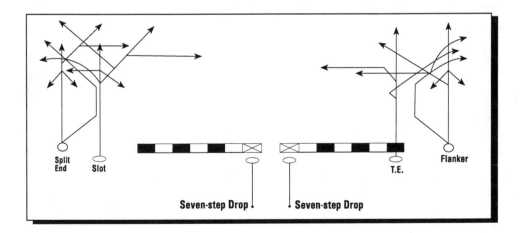

DRILL #37: OUTSIDE STREAK PASS DRILL

Objective: To isolate the ability to practice and execute the outside streak pass route.

Equipment Needed: Six footballs; lined field.

Description: Off of three-, five- or seven-stepped timed throws (depending on the offense used), the quarterback practices deep outside streak pass throws to his wide receivers. Two sets of quarterbacks and wide receivers can go at the same time. The quarterbacks should be sure to practice their deep streak throws equally to the right and left. Left hash, right hash, and middle of the field considerations should be made.

Coaching Points:

- The quarterback should use his sideline spacing to properly drop the ball into his wide receivers.

- The football must be kept in-bounds.

- The coach should check for proper plant throw, plant pop-up, plant hitch-up or play action stepping, according to the offense used.

- The quarterback should be sure to follow through to the zenith (highest) point of the streak pass to get the football to properly turn over, nose down, as it descends to the receiver.

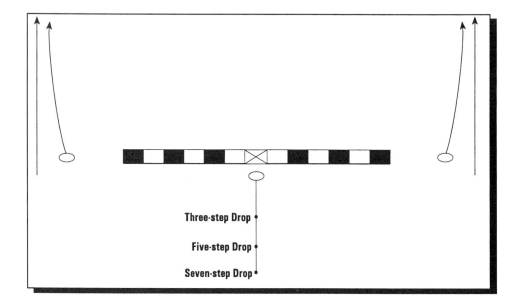

DRILL #38: ONE-ON-ONE STREAK PASS DRILL

Objective: To coordinate the practice of properly thrown outside streak passes to a wide receiver covered one-on-one by a pass defender.

Equipment Needed: Six footballs; lined field.

Description: This drill is run in the same fashion as the Outside Streak Pass Drill with the exception that a defensive back is covering streak throws. This competitive drill teaches the quarterback the importance of proper pass delivery timing, keeping the thrown football in-bounds and proper turn-over of the football so that the football drops in to the wide receiver. Even though the defender knows it's a streak pass, what is important is who makes the catch. Left hash, right hash and middle of the field adjustments should be made.

Coaching Points:

- The quarterback should properly use his sideline spacing to properly drop the ball into his wide receivers.

- The football must be kept in-bounds.

- The coach should check for proper plant throw, plant pop-up, plant hitch-up or play action stepping, according to the offense used.

- The quarterback should be sure to follow through to the zenith (highest) point of the streak pass to get the football to properly turn over, nose down, as it descends to the receiver.

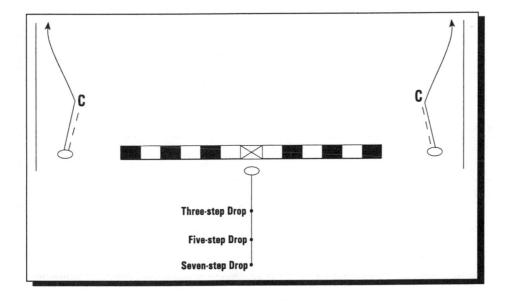

DRILL #39: SCREEN PASS DRILL

Objective: To practice the mechanics of screen passing.

Equipment Needed: One football per quarterback; line-spacing tapes or hoses.

Description: Versus a defensive end/rush outside linebacker, the quarterback takes a five-step drop to draw the rusher to him, resets for two steps and delivers a screen pass to his back (slot, tight end, etc.). The quarterback should practice whatever screen actions his offense utilizes.

Coaching Points:

- This drill is as helpful to the screen receiver as it is to the quarterback.

- The quarterback should learn to be an "athlete" in this drill. He should get the football to the screen receiver no matter what type of rush he is experiencing. He may have to lift his throwing platform (high hold of football) up high, jump pass, sidearm pass, etc.

- Since the quarterback may not be able to utilize a good throwing base as a result of rush evasion, index finger follow through should be emphasized.

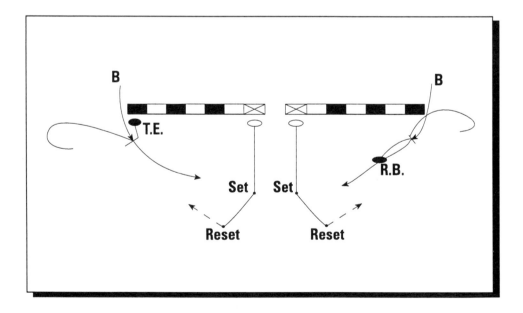

DRILL #40: LAST-PHASE INDIVIDUAL ROUTE PASS DRILL

Objective: To practice passing to specific routes by the receivers.

Equipment Needed: Eight to ten footballs; spacing tape or hose.

Description: This drill isolates the timing of the last portion of a route. The receivers position themselves downfield at the point of the route called by the coach at which the final break will be made. The receiver watches the quarterback in a ready stance and executes the final break of the route as he sees the quarterback plant his foot at the end of his drop-back action. The last-phase concept can be added to any timed route passing action or to any of the previously discussed individual route passing drills.

Coaching Points:

- This drill can be used before practice for extra passing and receiving timing work without tiring the receivers before the actual practice starts.

- The coach should be sure that the receivers are positioned properly for each route to enable a proper practice of that route and its timing.

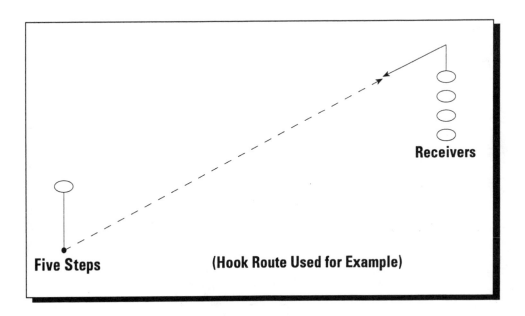

DRILL #41: BALLS-IN-THE-AIR DRILL

Objective: To rapid-fire practice all of the pass route throws of a particular offense and get as many repetitions completed as possible in a given time period.

Equipment Needed: 15 to 20 footballs; spacing tapes or hoses; lined field.

Description: From preconceived formation sets, the quarterbacks (or coach) point to a receiver and call out the particular route to be run. The quarterback who is "up" throws the particular route called. All quarterbacks alternate the throwing from the left and right side as they mill over the center area awaiting a football from the manager. "Rapid fire" passing and catching is emphasized. Left hash, right hash and middle of the field adjustments should be made.

Coaching Points:

- The coach should be sure that all of the types of routes in the offense (back, tight end, wide receiver, short, intermediate and deep) are being practiced.

- The coach should start with shorter routes and work up to intermediate and deep routes as the quarterbacks' arms warm up.

- The key to the drill is having lots of balls in the air so that lots of passes and catches are made.

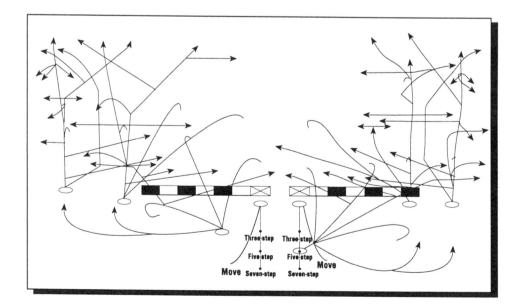

DRILL #42: INDIVIDUAL RED ZONE PASS ROUTE DRILL

Objective: To learn and practice the specific passes of an offense's Red Zone pass attack.

Equipment Needed: Eight to ten footballs; lined spacing tape or hose; lined field (Red Zone area).

Description: From preconceived formation sets, and off of three-, five-, or seven-step timed drops (or any other drop back, move, sprint-out, roll-out or play action), the quarterbacks practice their individual Red Zone pass routes passing to all receiving positions at the same time. A manager should assist in the return of the footballs so that as many passes can be thrown as possible in the allotted time period. Throws should be made equally to the left and right. Left hash, right hash, and middle of the field considerations should be taken into account.

Coaching Points:

- In the Red Zone (30, 25, or 20 yard line in), man route throw considerations (anti-blitz) should be made in regard to the specific routes utilized in the offense and in the way that the routes are thrown to (lead the man-breaking routes with the throws).

- Practicing the Red Zone route throws on a lined field in the actual Red Zone area helps to create specificity of practice.

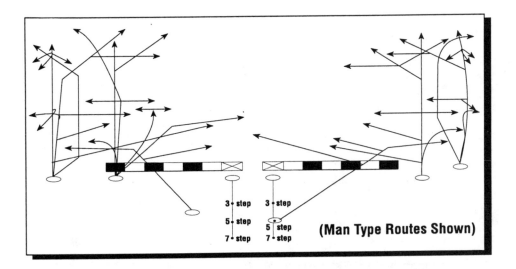

3-step	3-step
5-step	5-step
7-step	7-step

(Man Type Routes Shown)

DRILL #43: INDIVIDUAL GOAL LINE PASS ROUTE DRILL

Objective: To learn and practice the specific passes of an offense's goal line pass attack.

Equipment Needed: Eight to ten footballs; line-spacing tape or hose; lined field (goal line area).

Description: From preconceived formation sets, and off of three-, five-, or seven-step timed drops (or any other drop back, move, sprint-out, roll-out or play action), the quarterbacks practice their individual goal line pass route passing to all receiving positions at the same time. A manager should assist in the return of the footballs so that as many passes can be thrown as possible in the allotted time period. Throws should be made equally to the left and right. Left hash, right hash, and middle of the field considerations should be made.

Coaching Points:

- The routes thrown to must come from the specific routes executed in the offense's specific goal line pass attack. Proper goal line area spacing of all routes is essential.

- A lined goal line area should be utilized to help create specificity of practice, as well as flags (cones) placed for the end line hash-mark flag, the corner end zone flag and the goal line flag.

- Man coverage end zone route considerations should be taken into account.

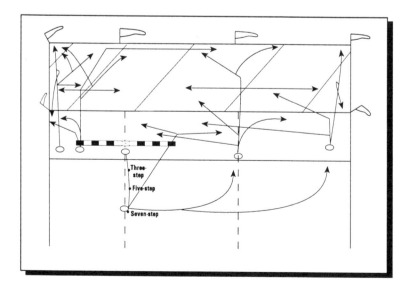

DRILL #44: BACKFIELD/TIGHT END HOT/DUMP DRILL

Objective: To practice Hot/Dump-type passing to the backs and tight ends versus inside and outside linebacker/strong safety-type blitzing.

Equipment Needed: One football per quarterback; spacing tape or hose; mechanical snapper.

Description: Versus simulated inside/outside linebacker and strong safety blitz looks, the quarterback practices throwing to the anti-blitz routes of the backs and tight ends in his particular offense.

Coaching Points:

- The coach should ensure specificity of practice by using the Hot/Dump blitz-beater routes of his backs and tight ends in his particular offense.

- The quarterback should be ready to throw dump pass routes by the third step of his drop.

- Since the quarterback is dropping back and falling away from his throw, he should raise his throwing platform (high hold of the football) to ensure an over-the-top throw and utilize extra index finger follow-through.

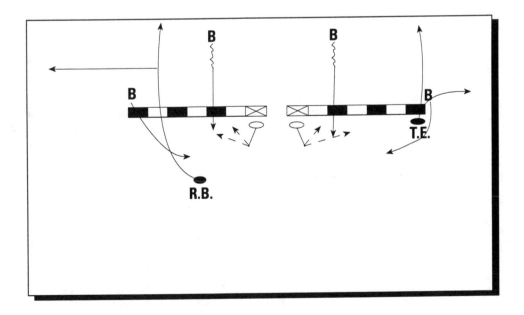

DRILL #45: SPREAD RECEIVER HOT/DUMP DRILL

Objective: To practice Hot/Dump-type passing to the spread receivers versus inside and outside linebacker/strong safety-type blitzing.

Equipment Needed: One football per quarterback; line-spacing tape or hose; mechanical snapper.

Description: Versus simulated inside and outside linebacker/strong safety blitz looks, the quarterback practices throwing to the anti-blitz routes of the spread receivers in his particular offense.

Coaching Points:

- This drill is limited to those passing offenses that utilize spread receiver Hot/Dump-type anti-blitz control routes versus inside and outside linebacker/strong safety-type blitzes.

- The quarterback should be ready to throw such hot/dump pass-type routes by the third step of his drop.

- Since the quarterback is dropping back and falling away from his throw, he should raise his throwing platform (high hold of football) to ensure an over-the-top throw and utilize extra index finger follow-through.

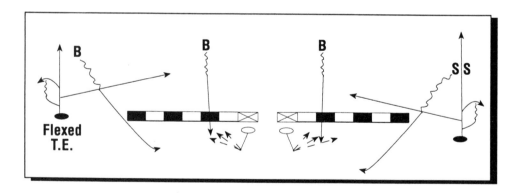

DRILL #46: SPREAD RECEIVER HOT/SIGHT ADJUST DRILL

Objective: To practice Hot/Sight Adjust-type passing to the spread receivers versus secondary blitzes.

Equipment Needed: One football per quarterback; line-spacing tape or hose; mechanical snapper.

Description: Versus simulated secondary blitz looks, the quarterback practices throwing to the anti-blitz routes of the spread receivers his particular offense.

Coaching Points:

- The coach should ensure specificity of practice by using the Hot/Sight Adjust blitz-beater routes of his particular offense.

- The quarterback should be ready to throw such hot/dump pass-type routes by the third step of his drop.

- Since the quarterback is dropping back and falling away from his throw, he should raise his throwing platform (high hold of football) to ensure an over-the-top throw and utilize extra index finger follow-through.

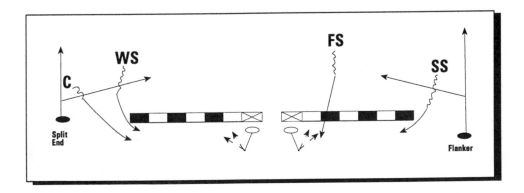

DRILL #47: SKELETON PASS HOT/DUMP/SIGHT ADJUST DRILL

Objective: To practice all Hot/Dump/Sight Adjust-type passing versus all inside and outside linebacker/strong safety and secondary blitzes.

Equipment Needed: One football per quarterback; line-spacing tape or hose; mechanical snapper.

Description: This drill is set up as a full seven-on-seven (or eight-on-seven) skeleton pass drill. However, all emphasis is on blitz control with all of the Hot/Dump/Sight Adjust blitz control routes used by the team's particular offense. Some type of blitz (and blitz control throw) is executed on every repetition.

Coaching Points:

- This drill combines all of the blitz control-type passing utilized by the team's particular offense. The blitzes are continually mixed to force the quarterback to utilize all of his anti-blitz throws.

- The quarterback should be ready to throw such hot/dump pass-type routes by the third step of his drop.

- Since the quarterback is dropping back and falling away from his throw, he should raise his throwing platform (high hold of football) to ensure an over-the-top throw and utilize extra index finger follow through.

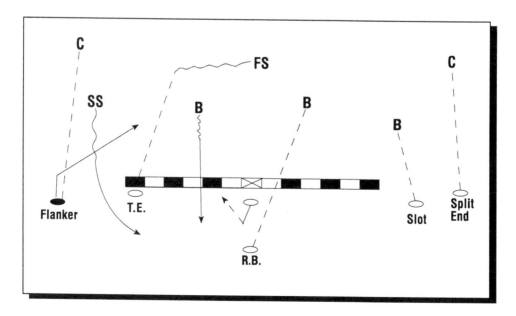

DRILL #48: HI / LO READ PASS DRILL

Objective: To practice the all-important skill of making a correct Hi/Lo read on a defender and a resultant proper pass to the open Hi/Lo receiver.

Equipment Needed: Three to four footballs; lined field.

Description: Off of designated Hi/Lo pattern read action from the team's actual pass offense, the quarterback takes his normal drop back or play action set, reads the drop of a cornerback, strong safety type defender or linebacker and throws to the proper Hi or Lo receiver according to the defender's drop.

Coaching Points:

- The coach should check for proper set-up action, be it drop back, play action, etc.

- If the defender being read is Hi, the quarterback throws Lo. If the defender stays Lo, the quarterback throws Hi.

- If in doubt, the quarterback should always throw Lo.

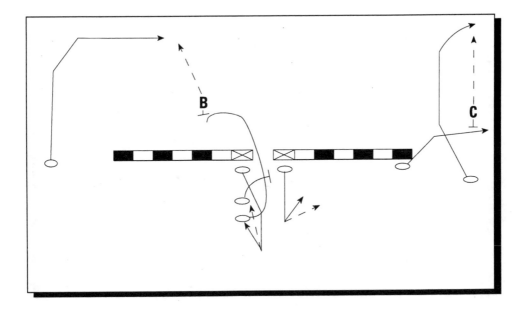

DRILL #49: LATERAL READ PASS DRILL

Objective: To practice making a correct Lateral read on a defender and a proper pass to the open Lateral read receiver.

Equipment Needed: Three to four footballs; lined field.

Description: Off of designated Lateral pattern read action from the team's actual pass offense, the quarterback takes his normal drop back or play action set, reads the drop of an underneath coverage defender (linebacker, strong safety) and throws to the open Lateral receiver according to the defender's drop.

Coaching Points:

- The coach should check for proper set-up action, be it drop back, play action, etc.

- If the defender being read drops to the outside, the quarterback throws to the inside receiver. If the defender stays inside, the quarterback throws outside.

- If in doubt, the quarterback should throw to the nearer, inside receiver.

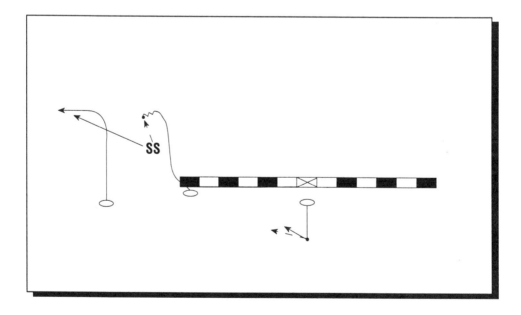

DRILL #50: MIDDLE LATERAL READ PASS DRILL

Objective: To practice making a correct inside or middle 3-on-2 Lateral read action on two inside linebackers and a proper pass to the open Middle Lateral read receiver.

Equipment Needed: Three to four footballs; lined field.

Description: Off of designated Middle (or Inside) Lateral read action from the team's actual pass offense, the quarterback takes his normal drop back or play action set, reads the middle receiver to see the peripheral drops of the inside linebackers and throws to the open receiver of the three.

Coaching Points:

- The coach should check for proper set-up action, be it drop back, play action, etc.

- The quarterback initially reads the middle receiver. If he is open, the quarterback throws to him. If there is coverage color on the middle receiver from the left, the quarterback throws to the left receiver. If there is coverage color from the right, the quarterback throws to the right receiver.

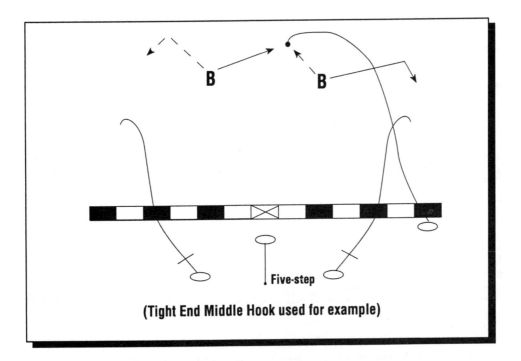

(Tight End Middle Hook used for example)

DRILL #51: INSIDE ONE-ON-ONE PASS DRILL

Objective: To practice passing to all of the routes of the backs, tight ends and wing/tight slot receivers versus the man coverage of the inside and outside linebackers, strong safeties and nickel defenders.

Equipment Needed: Three to four footballs; line-spacing tape or hose; lined field.

Description: From normal formation alignments, the quarterbacks throw to the routes of the backs, tight ends and wing/slot receivers versus the man coverage of the inside and outside linebackers, strong safeties and nickel defenders. The quarterbacks and receivers should also work versus a variety of bump/press/tight/loose/off man coverages. Since the receivers may break inside or outside according to the man coverage, only one quarterback-receiver-defender set can go at a time. The next group should be ready to go immediately.

Coaching Points:

- The coach should be sure to practice all possible routes versus the man coverage, utilizing all necessary man coverage adjustments.

- The quarterback should be sure to lead the receivers away from man coverage after the receivers make their man coverage separation technique breaks.

- The coach should be sure to practice the man routes and throw executions versus bump/press/tight/loose/off man coverages.

- The coach can start all of the repetitions from a yard line (50, 40, 30, etc.) and challenge the receivers to score on each repetition to practice open field running and defensive pursuit. The yardage statistics can be charted.

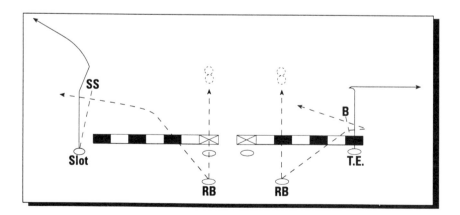

DRILL #52: OUTSIDE ONE-ON-ONE PASS DRILL

Objective: To practice passing to all of the routes of the wide receivers, wide slot and spread tight end receivers versus the man coverage of the cornerbacks, safeties, and nickel and dime coverage defenders.

Equipment Needed: Three to four footballs; line-spacing tape or hose; lined field.

Description: From normal formation alignments, the quarterbacks throw to the routes of the wide receivers, wide slots and spread tight end receivers versus the man coverage of the cornerbacks, safeties and nickel and dime coverage defenders. The quarterbacks and receivers should also work versus the variety of bump/press/tight/loose/off man coverages. Since the receivers may break inside or outside according to the man coverage, only one quarterback-receiver-defender set can go at a time. The next group should be ready to go immediately.

Coaching Points:

- The coach should be sure to practice all possible routes versus the man coverage, utilizing all necessary man coverage adjustments.

- The quarterback should be sure to lead the receivers away from man coverage after the receivers make their man coverage separation technique breaks.

- The coach should be sure to practice the man route and throw execution versus bump/press/tight/loose/off man coverages.

- The coach can start all of the repetitions from a yard line (50, 40, 30, etc.) and challenge the receivers to score on each repetition to practice open field running and defensive pursuit. The yardage statistics can be charted.

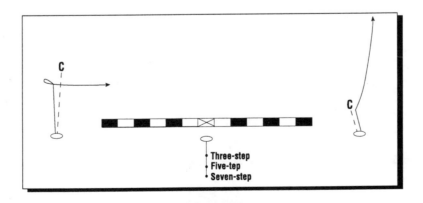

DRILL #53: LINE PASS UNDER PRESSURE DRILL

Objective: To progress from skeleton pass work to full-team offense-defense pass work with line pressure being put on the quarterbacks from the defensive line's rush.

Equipment Needed: One football; lined field.

Description: This drill is a live, eleven-on-eleven, offense versus defense drill. However, the only live rush that the quarterback and the rest of the offense receives is from the three, four, or five defensive linemen. Any twist, slant or angle stunts can be utilized.

Coaching Points:

- The emphasis is on the pass. However, occasional pass complementary runs (draw, trap, draw trap, shovel pass) can be utilized to counteract the heavy pass rush threats by the defensive line.

- This drill is much more realistic for the quarterback because he is forced to learn to read and throw versus the variety of coverages he may see with a live defensive line rush in front of him.

- This drill can be a thud drill or used in a live scrimmage setting. However, no live contact should be made on a quarterback wearing a red shirt.

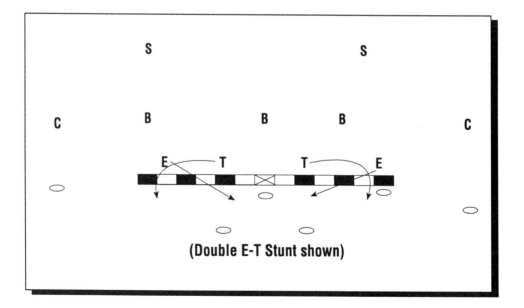

(Double E-T Stunt shown)

DRILL #54: FRONT PASS UNDER PRESSURE DRILL

Objective: To progress from skeleton pass work and defensive line only full pass pressure to full-team offensive-defensive pass work with live pressure being put on the quarterbacks with the defensive fronts stunt and blitz pressure package.

Equipment Needed: One football; line field.

Description: This drill is a live, eleven-on-eleven, offense versus defense team drill. However, the live rush that the quarterback, and the rest of the offense, receives is from the front only. Any combination of front slant, angle, twist, or linebacker/ strong safety blitz can be utilized.

Coaching Points:

- The emphasis is on the pass. However, occasional complementary runs (draw, trap, draw trap, shovel pass) can be utilized to counteract the heavy pass rush threats by the defensive front.

- This drill is a much more realistic for the quarterback because he is forced to learn to read and throw versus the variety of coverages he may see with a live defensive front rush in front of him.

- This drill can be a thud drill or used in a live scrimmage setting. However, no live contact should be made on a quarterback wearing a red shirt.

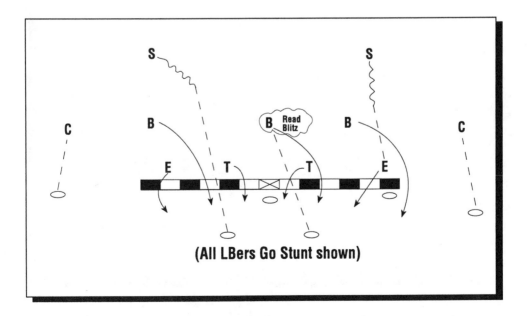

(All LBers Go Stunt shown)

DRILL #55: FULL BLITZ PASS UNDER PRESSURE DRILL

Objective: To progress from skeleton pass work and defensive line and defensive front only pass pressure to full-team offensive-defensive pass work with live pressure being put on the quarterback's from the entire defense's stunt and blitz pressure package.

Equipment Needed: One football; lined field.

Description: This drill is a live, eleven-on-eleven, offense versus defense team drill. The offense, however, can now receive the full complement of defensive line, front and secondary stunts and blitzes in any combination.

Coaching Points:

- The emphasis is on the pass. However, occasional pass complementary runs (draw, trap, draw trap, shovel pass) can be utilized to counteract the heavy pass rush threats by the defense.

- This drill is much more realistic for the quarterback because he is forced to learn to read and throw versus the variety of coverages he may see with a live defensive stunt and blitz package in front of him.

- This drill can be a thud drill or used in a live scrimmage setting. However, no live contact should be made on a quarterback wearing a red shirt.

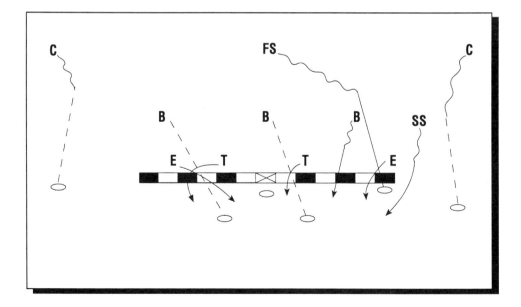

DRILL #56: UNIT BREAKDOWN PASS DRILL

Objective: To focus on the isolation aspect of a specific part of a pattern, the defensive coverages it could face and the subsequent defensive key reads the quarterback will have to make.

Equipment Needed: Three to four footballs; a line-spacing tape or hose.

Description: In this drill, the receivers execute their pass routes. Thus, the quarterback gets the opportunity to read the defensive coverage and also the receivers' routes in relation to the coverages. The drill is a game-like enactment of an isolated part of the passing game versus a variety of coverages.

Coaching Points:

- The quarterback should anticipate his throw possibilities before the football is even snapped (or simulation of the snap).

- The quarterback should focus on his key reads as he sets up.

- The quarterback should be aware of the possible receiver adjustments to coverages if the pass pattern allows for such route adjustments.

- This drill can be modified to isolate on the prime read aspect of a specific pattern only.

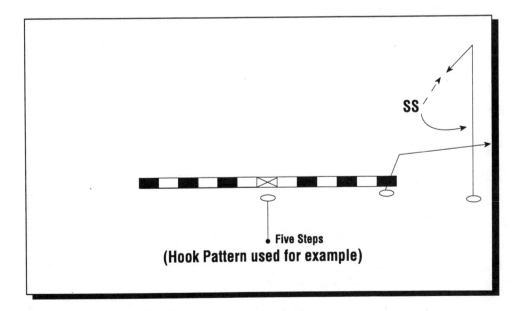

Five Steps
(Hook Pattern used for example)

DRILL #57: HALF SKELETON PASS DRILL

Objective: To focus on and practice the playside prime routes and reads of a particular pattern or the backside outlet routes in a half-field, half-skeleton practice situation.

Equipment Needed: Two footballs; one or two spacing tapes or hoses; lined field.

Description: Using normal formation sets, the offense pits the quarterback and one side (one half) of its wide receivers, tight ends, wings, slots, and backs against one side (one half) of the defense's linebackers, safeties, cornerbacks, and nickel and dime personnel, executing the team's pass offense. Normal left hash, right hash, and middle of the field considerations are taken into account. Designated varieties of coverage (man, zone, two deep, three deep, combo/blitz/man free, etc.) are utilized.

Coaching Points:

- If the offense is using the frontside, prime portion of the particular pattern, some form of backside outlet or dump should be provided so the quarterback is not left stranded if the prime routes are covered (a manager will do).

- If the quarterback is working the backside outlet portion of the pattern, he should enact an imaginary sequencing of the entire pattern (the prime route reads initially) so he can work to his outlet routes with proper timing.

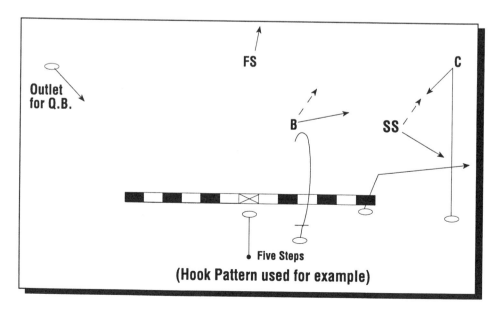

(Hook Pattern used for example)

DRILL #58: MIDDLE SKELETON PASS DRILL

Objective: To focus on and practice any backfield, tight end, tight slot or wing patterns and routes that work on the middle, underneath area coverage of a defense, be it zone or man.

Equipment Needed: One football; spacing tape or hose; lined field.

Description: Using normal formation sets, the offense pits the quarterback and the inside receivers (backs, tight ends, tight slots and wings) against the inside and outside linebackers and strong safeties. Patterns that concentrate on using routes by the inside receivers to attack this underneath, interior coverage defenders are utilized. In essence, the drill becomes an inside 2-on-3, 3-on-3, or 3-on-4 Middle Pass Skeleton Drill. Normal left hash, right hash and middle of the field considerations are taken into account. Designated varieties of coverage (man, zone, two deep, three deep, inside/outside zone combo, etc.) are utilized.

Coaching Points:

- The drill can involve fast-paced first team versus first team work, or, scout squad personnel can be utilized to simulate an opposing team's underneath, inside coverage.

- The coach should keep in mind the need to work against any inside blitzes or stunts by the linebackers or strong safeties.

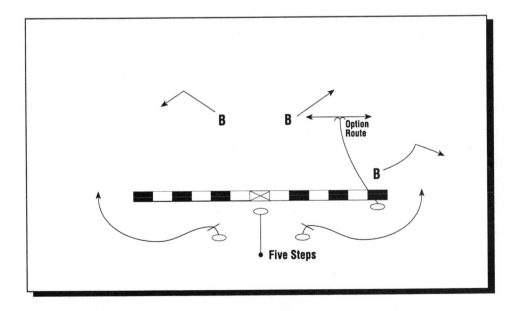

DRILL #59: SKELETON PASS DRILL

Objective: To practice the reads and subsequent passes of one's specific pass offense versus designated coverages of the defense.

Equipment Needed: Two footballs; line-spacing tape or hose; lined field.

Description: Using normal formation sets, the offense pits its quarterback, wide receivers, tight ends, wings, slots, and backs against the defense's linebackers, safeties, cornerbacks and nickel and dime personnel, executing the team's pass attack. Normal left hash, right hash and middle of the field considerations are taken into account. Designated varieties of coverage (man, zone, two deep, three deep/blitz/combo/man free, etc.) are utilized.

Coaching Points:

- Fast paced "good-on-good" work in which the first offense is pitted against the first defense helps to create an excellent game-like pace. However, the offense is then limited to the defense's specific coverages.

- Working versus a scout team defense enables the offense to practice versus the designated coverages it needs to work against in preparation for a game.

- The coach should be sure that the quarterback (and rest of the pass offense) works against a significant amount of blitzes in the drill.

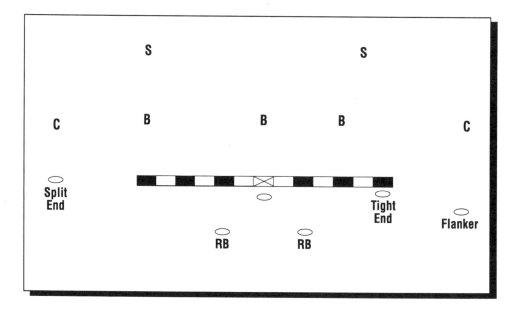

DRILL #60: 3RD DOWN SKELETON PASS DRILL

Objective: To practice all of the reads and subsequent passes of one's specific third-down pass offense versus designated third-down coverages of the defense.

Equipment Needed: Two footballs; line-spacing tape or hose; lined field.

Description: Using normal third-down formation sets, the offense pits its quarterback, wide receivers, tight ends, wings, slots, and backs against the defense's linebackers, safeties, cornerbacks and nickel and dime personnel, executing the team's third-down pass attack. Normal left hash, right hash and middle of the field considerations are taken into account as well as third and short, medium and long down and distance coverage considerations. Designated varieties of coverage (man, zone, two deep, three deep/blitz/combo/man free, etc.) are utilized. The situations (3rd and 2, 5, 7, 9, 11, 13, etc.) are called out before each repetition.

Coaching Points:

- Fast-paced "good-on-good" work in which the first offense is pitted against the first defense helps to create an excellent game-like pace, but limits the offense to the defense's specific coverages. Working versus a scout team defense enables the offense to practice versus the designated coverages it will face in a game.

- The coach should be sure that the quarterback (and rest of the pass offense) works against a significant amount of blitzes in the drill.

- To help expedite the drill, the coach may want to devote a complete time period block (five minutes) per down and distance situation (3rd and 5).

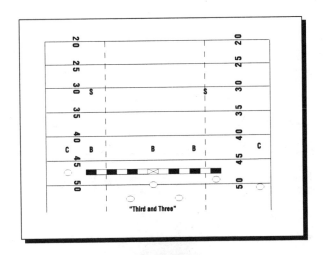

"Third and Three"

DRILL #61: RED ZONE SKELETON PASS DRILL

Objective: To practice all of the reads and subsequent passes of one's specific Red Zone pass offense versus designated Red Zone coverages of the defense.

Equipment Needed: Two footballs; line-spacing tape or hose; lined field.

Description: Using normal Red Zone formation sets, the offense pits its quarterback, wide receivers, tight ends, wings, slots, and backs against the defense's linebackers, safeties, cornerbacks and nickel and dime personnel, executing the team's Red Zone pass attack. Normal left hash, right hash and middle of the field considerations are taken into account as well as all Red Zone pressure and blitz coverage considerations. Designated varieties of coverage (man, zone, two deep, three deep/blitz/combo/man free, etc.) are utilized.

Coaching Points:

- Fast-paced "good-on-good" work in which the first offense is pitted against the first defense helps to create an excellent game-like pace, but limits the offense to the defense's specific coverages. Working versus a scout team defense enables the offense to practice versus the designated coverages it will face in a game.

- The coach should be sure that the quarterback (and rest of the pass offense) works against a significant amount of blitzes in the drill.

- To help expedite the drill, the coach may want to devote a complete time block (five minutes) per yard line (+25, +20, +17, +12, +8, etc.).

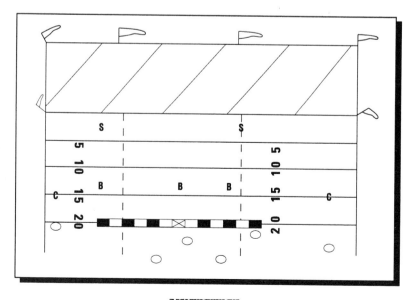

DRILL #62: GOAL LINE ROUTE SPACING DRILL

Objective: To practice the execution of the specific goal line patterns and routes of one's offense in the limited goal line area.

Equipment Needed: One football; spacing tape or hose; lined goal line area.

Description: The offense runs and executes its specific goal line pass patterns "on air" (without defenders). The coach can designate a specific route for the quarterback to throw to, or he himself (or a manager) can act to simulate the prime read of the pattern. The practice of the route spacing in the limited goal line area, using the hash end line flags, the corner end line flags and the end zone corner flags receives the primary emphasis.

Coaching Points:

- The drill gives the quarterback the different "feel" for the specific goal line patterns in the limited goal line area as they develop in front of him.

- Man and zone route running considerations should be included.

- The quarterback should also execute any line of scrimmage/goal line run threat attack that may be a part of his offense's goal line attack (sprint-out, roll-out, bootleg, waggle, play action, etc.).

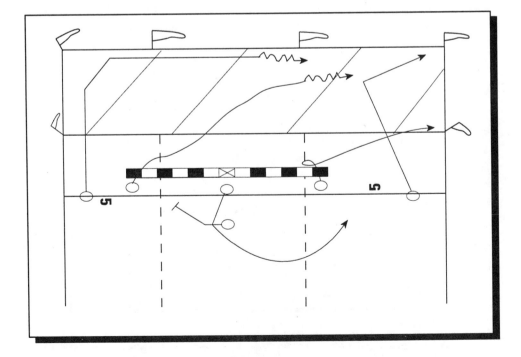

DRILL #63: GOAL LINE SKELETON PASS DRILL

Objective: To practice all of the reads and subsequent passes of one's specific goal line pass offense versus designated goal line coverages of the defense.

Equipment Needed: Two footballs; line-spacing tape or hose; lined field.

Description: Using normal goal line formation sets, the offense pits its quarterback, wide receivers, tight ends, wings, slots, and backs against the defense's linebackers, safeties, cornerbacks and nickel and dime personnel, executing the team's goal line pass attack. Normal left hash, right hash and middle of the field considerations are taken into account as well as all goal line pressure and blitz coverage considerations. Designated varieties of goal line coverage (man, zone, blitz, etc.) are utilized.

Coaching Points:

• This drill is a very difficult for the offense since there is a limited number of vertical yards to work in. Conversely, the defense is not worrying about runs, so their pass coverage abilities are not limited.

• Precise route running and distribution is essential in the limited goal line area.

• The coach should be sure the quarterback and the pass offense are working versus the specific goal line coverages and blitzes they will see in this area of the field.

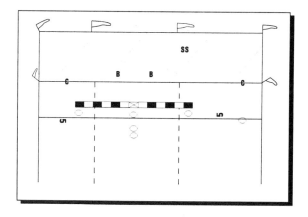

DRILL #64: TWO-MINUTE ON AIR DRILL

Objective: To teach, practice and execute the quarterback's two-minute offense mechanics.

Equipment Needed: One football; lined field.

Description: This drill emphasizes communication. A second quarterback spots the ball on the five yard line coming out on either hash or in the middle of the field. The quarterback executing the drill calls out the proper two-minute offensive formation in relation to the field position. He then looks to the coach/other quarterback on the sideline to get the play call, barks out the play signal to both sides of the formation and calls the two-minute snap count cadence. The quarterback then throws the ball to the "spotter," who moves the ball to the next five yard line as he constantly adjusts the field position of the ball. The drill is executed all the way down the field with the same quarterback.

Coaching Points:

- The coach should mix all of the two-minute offense play calls up and down the field.

- Team two-minute offense execution is as much the quarterback's ability to get the offense in proper formation and get the line of scrimmage play communicated as anything else.

- Quarterbacks can practice this drill during kicking game periods if they are not involved.

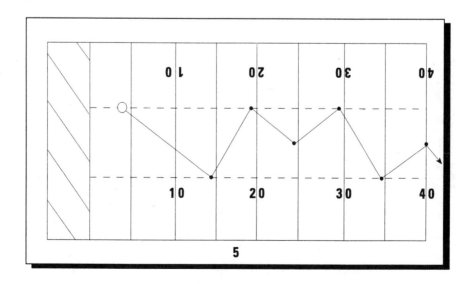

CHAPTER 2

OPTION DRILLS

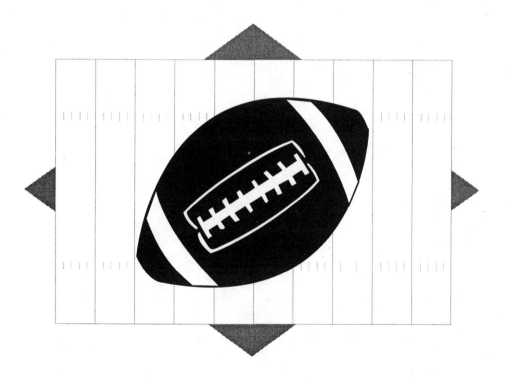

DRILL #65: KNEELING PITCH DRILL

Objective: To practice option pitching from a kneeling position.

Equipment Needed: One football per two quarterbacks.

Description: Two quarterbacks kneel in an approximate 45° angle positioning from one another to produce the desired pitch option ratio utilized by the quarterbacks' particular option offense. Thus, if the pitch-option ratio is four yards by four yards, then the quarterbacks kneel in a position that allows them to extend their hands to the four by four position. The quarterbacks practice pitching right handed for a set number of repetitions and then switch positioning to practice left-handed pitches.

Coaching Points:

- Pitches should start from the sternum, not the belt buckle area to help produce a soft tumble on the ball that drops into the hands of the pitch back.

- The thumb should rotate downward as the ball is released to produce a soft tumble of the ball.

- The pitching quarterback should follow through to the pitch spot with the palm of his hand. The palm should "take a picture" of the pitch spot.

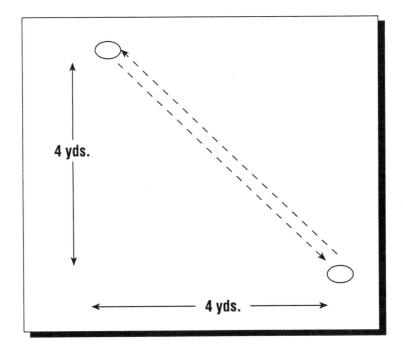

DRILL #66: DOWN-THE-LINE PITCH DRILL

Objective: To practice option pitching on-the-move.

Equipment Needed: One football per two quarterbacks; lined field.

Description: Two quarterbacks start on the sideline, one on a yard line and the other at a width (four yards, five yards) that will produce the width of the offense's pitch option ratio. The quarterback with the football jogs in place until the other quarterback runs out in front of him. When the receiving quarterback gets out in front of the pitching quarterback, the pitching quarterback begins to run and executes a proper option pitch of the ball. The receiving quarterback jogs in place until the other quarterback runs out in front of the jogging quarterback to reform the pitch ratio. The repetitions are repeated all the way across the field.

Coaching Points:

*   Pitches should start from the sternum, not the belt buckle area to help produce a soft tumble on the ball that drops into the hands of the pitch back.

*   The thumb should rotate downward as the ball is released to produce a soft tumble of the ball.

*   The pitching quarterback should follow through to the pitch spot with the palm of his hand. The palm should "take a picture" of the pitch spot.

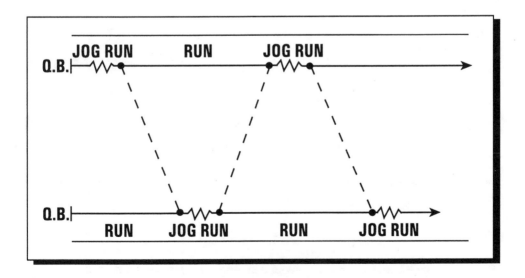

DRILL #67: DIVE OPTION DRILL

Objective: To practice two-on-one dive-keep option action on a defensive tackle.

Equipment Needed: One football; line-spacing tape or hose.

Description: Off of normally designed dive option action (inside dive, inside veer, freeze, counter dive, etc.), the quarterback reads his dive key to two-on-one option that defender.

Coaching Points:

- If the dive key read does not attack the dive back, the quarterback should give.

- If the dive key attacks the dive back, the quarterback should pull the football and continue to attack the pitch-keep option defender.

- On ride-and-decide action, the football should only be ridden to the quarterback's belt buckle. Pulling the ball beyond that point is extremely dangerous.

- This drill can be utilized to dive-keep option an EOL defender on an outside veer-type action.

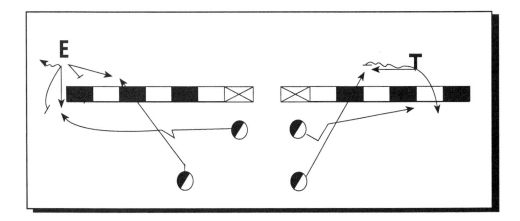

DRILL #68: END OF LINE OPTION PITCH DRILL

Objective: To practice two-on-one end-of-line pitch-keep option action on a defensive end/outside linebacker defender.

Equipment Needed: One football; line-spacing tape or hose.

Description: Off of normally designed option action (dive option, inside/outside veer, counter dive, trap, etc.), the quarterback attacks down the line of scrimmage to two-on-one option a defensive end/outside linebacker defender.

Coaching Points:

- The quarterback should work downhill into the LOS to put proper angle pressure on the EOL defender in an effort to make him commit to the quarterback's run threat. He should also attack at top speed so the EOL defender can't slow play the option action.

- The quarterback should execute proper pitch mechanics: pitching the football from the sternum, thumb down delivery for proper pitch rotation of the football and "taking-a-picture" with the palm of the hand to ensure proper follow through.

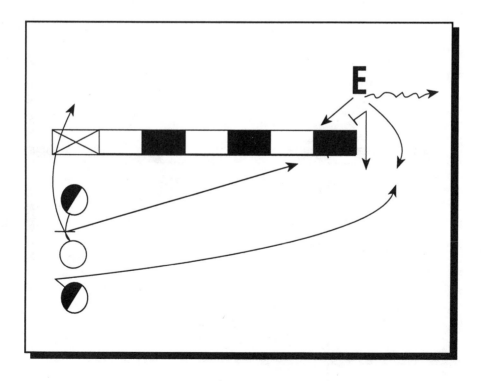

DRILL #69: OBSTACLE PITCH DRILL

Objective: To help the quarterback develop sound pitch skills when his pitch-option running action has been disturbed.

Equipment Needed: One football; two to three cones; two to three step-over bags; one hand shield; one spacing tape or hose.

Description: Off of designed option action (wishbone, inside dive, counter dive, etc.) the quarterback executes his pitch-keep option action off of artificially disturbed stepping action. The quarterback can be made to step over bags, around cones, be "bumped" by the coach with the shield or have a bag or shield thrown at his body.

Coaching Points:

- Whatever the obstacle, the quarterback should pitch from his sternum, properly rotate his thumb down and "take-a-picture" of the pitch point with the palm of his hand to ensure correct follow through.

- As the quarterback is being "disturbed," he should be concentrating on the positioning of his pitch back.

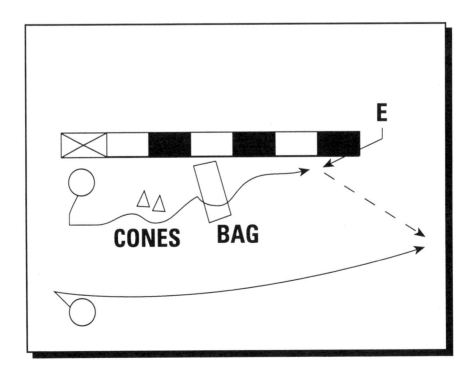

DRILL #70: PRESSURE PITCH DRILL

Objective: To help the quarterback develop sound pitch skills when he receives fast, hard outside pressure giving him a dangerous pitch read key.

Equipment Needed: One football; spacing tape or hose.

Description: Off of dive action or down-the-line option action (the coach or a simulated EOL defender), the quarterback pitches off a defender who is "in his face" right now. This drill helps the quarterback to be aware of such dangerous pitch option key action and to execute a proper pitch as a result.

Coaching Points:

- The quarterback should "ease off" with his body to help absorb the oncoming blow by the defender.

- The quarterback should realize that the pitch back will be much closer to him than normal and not as wide in his option ratio due to the necessity to pitch quickly on the extreme pressure. As a result, he should take "something off" the pitch, yet still follow through with the palm of his hand.

- The pitch back should also be aware of the fast, hard pressure. He should open his inside shoulder quickly to expect a quicker pitch.

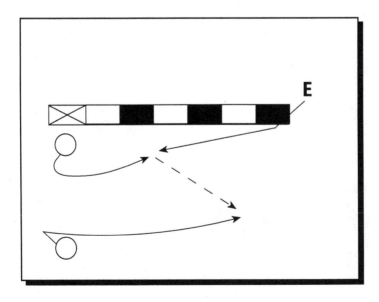

DRILL #71: DOWNFIELD OPTION PITCH DRILL

Objective: To practice downfield pitch-keep option action on a secondary defender once the quarterback has kept the ball at the LOS and is now attacking upfield into the secondary.

Equipment Needed: One football; line-spacing tape or hose.

Description: On any type of end-of-the-line option action, the coach, or simulated EOL defender works upfield to force the quarterback to initially keep the football. The quarterback now looks to pitch-keep option a secondary defender.

Coaching Points:

- The pitch back should hustle to create the downfield pitch option ratio (four to five yards wide and one yard behind the quarterback).

- The quarterback attacks the secondary defender. If the secondary defender commits to the quarterback, he pitches the football.

- The quarterback should remember this pitch action is just a little less than lateral to a pitch back who is now one yard behind him.

- Normal pitch execution mechanics should be stressed.

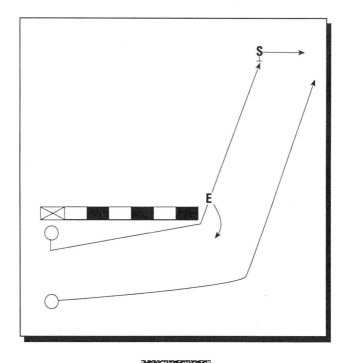

DRILL #72: RAPID FIRE OPTION PITCH DRILL

Objective: To practice a maximum amount of pitch-keep key reads and reactions and option pitches.

Equipment Needed: Two footballs; line-spacing tape or hose.

Description: Two quarterbacks work back and forth on a tape versus a simulated defensive end and carry out normal option actions. After each repetition, the quarterbacks switch roles as quarterback and pitchback. After two repetitions, the quarterbacks retrace the first two repetitions to practice the option action both left and right.

Coaching Points:

- The player simulating the defensive end varies his defensive option play on each repetition. The defender can sit, penetrate, crash, feather lightly, feather heavily, etc.

- The coach can jump in occasionally (or a second defender can be used) to create cross-charge situations.

- The coach should check all of the proper quarterback reactions to the defensive play (keep or pitch), plus proper pitching action.

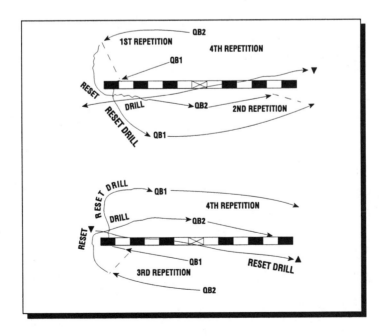

DRILL #73: MULTI-OPTION DRILL

Objective: To get maximum repetitions of the option plays used in one's offense.

Equipment Needed: Four footballs; two line-spacing tapes or hoses; lined field.

Description: Two tapes, or hoses, are set up with the center's "X" on the hash mark. A skeleton defense is set up utilizing those defenders needed to make all the necessary reads. Two offensive backfields are used to get maximum repetitions. The first repetition is started on the left tape and is an option play run into the sideline. All of the desired backfield option skills are checked. As the first backfield is finishing the play's execution, the second backfield sets up, and repeats the same play. As the second backfield is finishing its execution, the first backfield sets up to execute an option play to the right into the open field. When they finish, they set up on the tape on the right hash mark as the second backfield repeats the same play. After the first four repetitions from the left hash mark, the defenders switch to the tape on the right hash mark. Four option plays are run from each hash mark, two into the sideline and two into the wide side of the field. The plays are run in quick succession.

Coaching Points:

- The drill can be executed utilizing a noncontact action, or it can be run live or semi-live.

- Utilizing a second coach can help expedite the action of the defense.

- The drill should also be practiced with the tapes placed in various positions on the field.

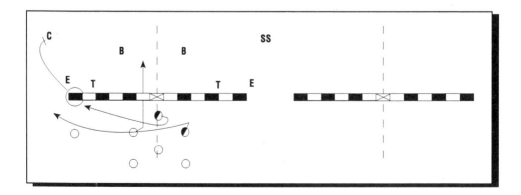

DRILL #74: CROSS-CHARGE OPTION DRILL

Objective: To practice all of the option plays of one's offense versus a wide variety of frontal and perimeter cross-charge stunts; to teach the quarterback to sort out exchanges of defensive assignments via cross-charge actions.

Equipment Needed: Two footballs; line-spacing tape or hose; lined field.

Description: Off of a line-spacing tape, the quarterback and backfield practice all of the option actions of their particular offense versus a variety of defensive cross-charge actions. Two offensive backfields are utilized to get maximum repetitions. The execution of the option plays versus cross-charges should be run both to the right and left.

Coaching Points:

- Since the quarterbacks are expecting cross-charge actions from the defense, it is important that a wide variety of cross-charge actions be utilized.

- The defense should use interior cross-charge stunts (linebacker/tackle cross-charge, tackle/end cross-charge, tackle-end pinch/linebacker loop cross-charge, etc.) as well as perimeter cross-charge stunts.

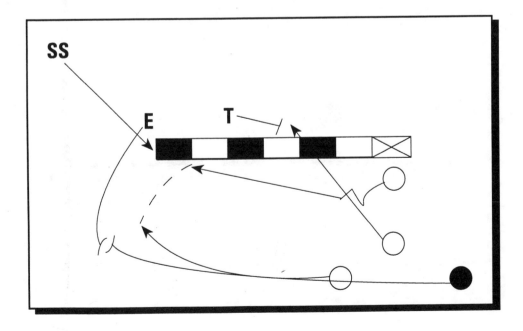

DRILL #75: TRIPLE OPTION DRILL

Objective: To practice three-on-two triple option dive-keep-pitch action on a dive and pitch option defender.

Equipment Needed: One football; line-spacing tape or hose.

Description: Off of normally designed triple-option action (dive, inside or outside veer, counter dive, wishbone), the quarterback reads and executes his dive key and then (if he hasn't handed the ball off to the dive back) reads and executes his pitch-keep key.

Coaching Points:

- The coaching points combine the coaching points of the Dive Option Drill and the End of Line Option Pitch Drill into one coordinated triple option action.

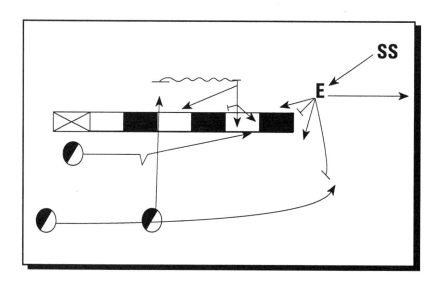

DRILL #76: PERIMETER OPTION DRILL

Objective: To practice the timing of the backfield option action with the perimeter blocks; to coordinate possible switching of blocking assignments of lead backs and wide receivers or inside receivers.

Equipment Needed: Two to three footballs; line-spacing tape or hose; lined field.

Description: All of the option plays used in a team's offense are practiced to both sides. Enough defenders are used to help create all the necessary option reads as well as to provide perimeter defenders for the perimeter blocking actions. To help create the proper play timing needed between the perimeter blocking schemes and the actual option action, the perimeter blocks should be executed as close to live action as possible.

Coaching Points:

- The coach should be sure to practice against a wide variety of defensive alignments and stunts.

- Cross-charge stunts should be included in the drill.

- The coach may want to include option play action passes to keep the defenders honest.

- Utilizing a second coach can help expedite the action of the defense.

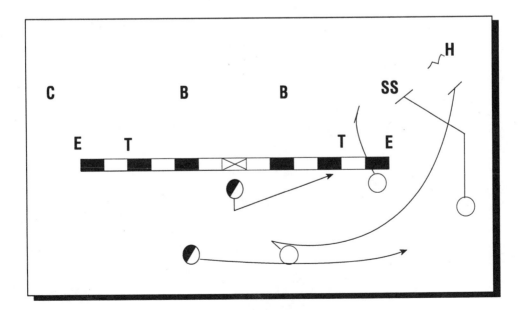

CHAPTER 3

EXCHANGE DRILLS

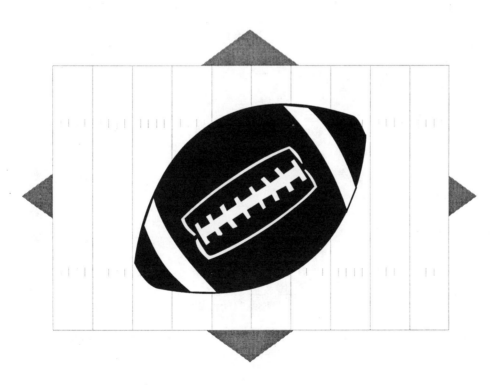

DRILL #77: RUN DELIVERY STEP DRILL

Objective: To practice the actual steps for the delivery of the football in the quarterback-ball carrier exchange according to the run plays in the offense.

Equipment Needed: One football per quarterback; lined field.

Description: The quarterbacks practice the steps of each run play in the offense "on-air." The coach can line his quarterbacks up so that they can all go at once or in "rapid-fire" order, one at a time.

Coaching Points:

- The coach should check for exact stepping action for both the run play exchange point and any faking action.

- The coach should be sure that the quarterback does not lift up and down during the stepping action so that a level, from the belt buckle exchange can be executed.

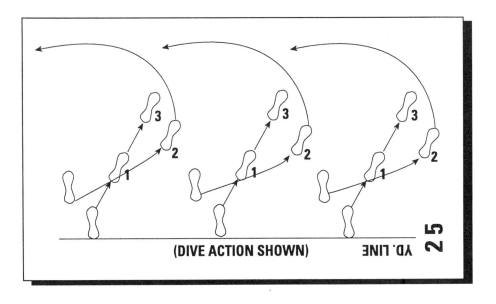

(DIVE ACTION SHOWN)   YD. LINE   2 5

DRILL #78: RUN TIMING DRILL

Objective: To practice the hand-off execution of all of the particular run plays in a team's offense.

Equipment Needed: One football per quarterback; a line-spacing tape or hose; a substitute or mechanical snapper.

Description: The quarterback executes all of the proper quarterback-ballcarrier exchange mechanics for the play called for by the coach. After each quarterback-ballcarrier exchange, the quarterback should execute proper play action pass or pitch-option fake action.

Coaching Points:

• The coach should check for proper stepping action to the mesh point.

• The quarterback should "deal" the football on the actual exchange from his own belt buckle. Holding the football up under the chin produces a downward angle delivery of the football which could hit the ball carrier's elbow as he forms his pouch.

• The quarterback should execute the exchange "on-the-money" two inches above the belly button, then fake.

• The quarterback should follow through on proper faking action after the exchange delivery.

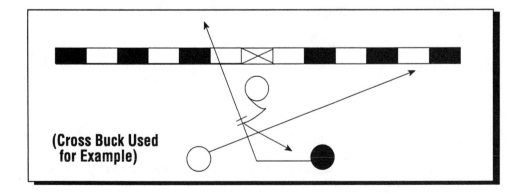

(Cross Buck Used for Example)

DRILL #79: PLAY ACTION TIMING DRILL

Objective: To practice the faking action of all play-action or option dive fakes.

Equipment Needed: One football per quarterback; a spacing tape or hose; a substitute or mechanical snapper.

Description: The quarterback executes all of the proper quarterback-back faking mechanics for the play called by the coach. The emphasis should be on great faking and then proper play action pass set-up action or pitch-keep option action.

Coaching Points:

- Proper one- or two-handed faking action of the ball should be emphasized.
- The coach should also emphasize proper play action pass set-up or option pitch-keep action after the fake.

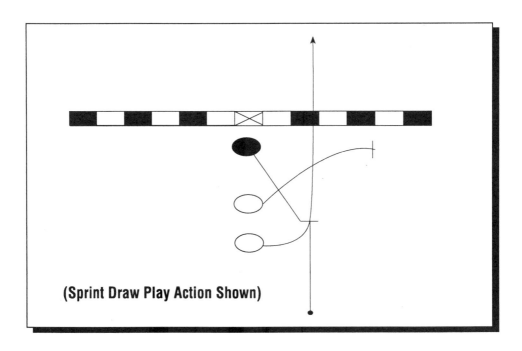

(Sprint Draw Play Action Shown)

DRILL #80: FOOL-THE-COACH DRILL

Objective: To blend actual play action run quarterback-ballcarrier exchange action and faking techniques so that they look like one another, helping to produce the most realistic and influencing of fakes.

Equipment Needed: One football per quarterback; a line-spacing tape or hose; a substitute or mechanical snapper.

Description: This drill is set up exactly like the Run Time Drill and the Play Action Timing Drill. The coach calls a series action (i.e., Sprint Draw) from a distance in front of the quarterback. The quarterback then whispers "Sprint Draw" or "Play Action" to his backs. The object is to execute all aspects of the run, the play action and the faking so well that the coach is fooled.

Coaching Points:

• The coach can give a 1 to 10 rating for each play based on how well the faking aspects of the play were achieved.

• This is a good drill can be videotaped from ground level to let the players grade themselves on how well they fake the play.

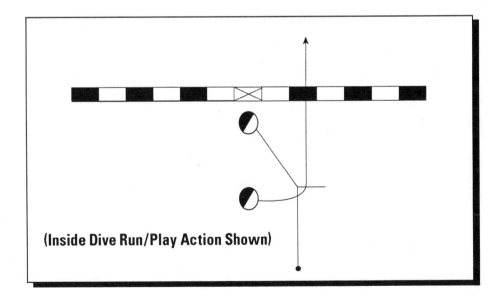

(Inside Dive Run/Play Action Shown)

CHAPTER 4

BALL DRILLS

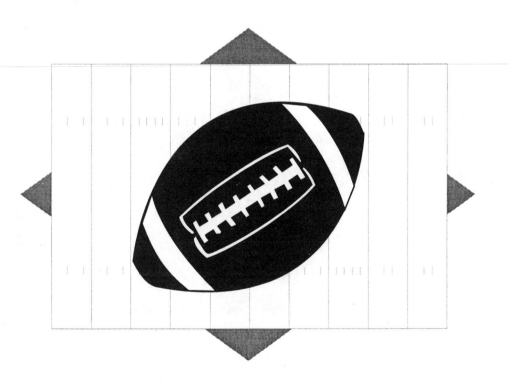

DRILL #81: AIR DRIBBLE DRILL

Objective: To develop gripping and re-gripping (catching) of the football.

Equipment Needed: One or two footballs per quarterback.

Description: The quarterback holds the football out in front of his body, drops the football, reaches down to catch-regrip it and pulls it back to the original hold position. The quarterback repeats the exercise as many times as he can in 30 seconds.

Coaching Points:

- The quarterback should work both hands equally.

- Once the quarterback becomes adept at the skill with both hands, two footballs can be used at the same time.

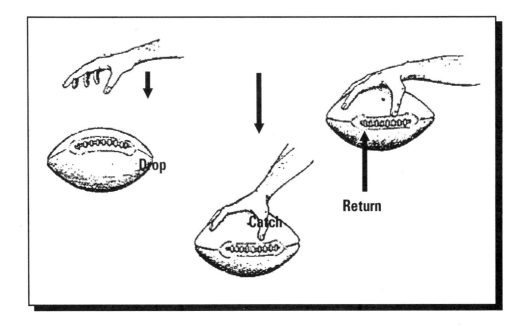

DRILL #82: GROUND DRIBBLE DRILL

Objective: To develop gripping and re-gripping (catching) skills of the football.

Equipment Needed: One or two footballs per quarterback.

Description: The Ground Dribble Drill is executed in the same fashion as the Air Dribble Drill except that the quarterback gets on a knee (or knees) and bounces or dribbles, the football off the ground. The quarterback repeats the exercise as many times as he can in 30 seconds.

Coaching Points:

- The quarterback should work both hands equally.
- Once the quarterback becomes adept at the skill with both hands, two footballs can be used at the same time.

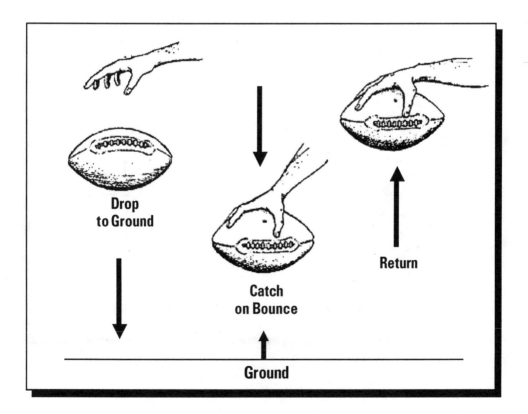

DRILL #83: FORWARD HAND ROLL DRILL

Objective: To develop adept football-handling skills.

Equipment Needed: One or two footballs per quarterback.

Description: The quarterback holds the football at one end with his palm facing down. The quarterback then rolls the football over his fingertips to the back of his hand with his palm still facing down. The quarterback then reverses the action to return it to its original position. The quarterback repeats the exercise as many times as he can in 30 seconds.

Coaching Points:

- The quarterback should work both hands equally.
- Once the quarterback becomes adept at the skill with both hands, two footballs can be used at the same time.

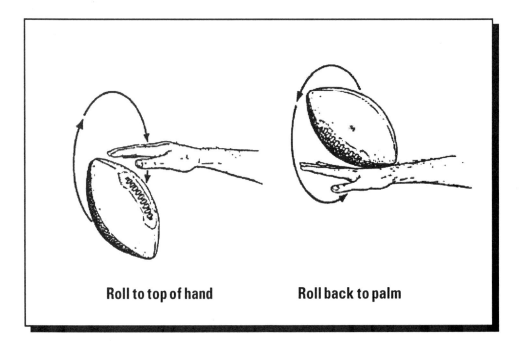

Roll to top of hand   **Roll back to palm**

DRILL #84: FORWARD FINGER FLIP DRILL

Objective: To develop adept football-handling skills.

Equipment Needed: One or two footballs per quarterback.

Description: The drill is executed in the same fashion as the Forward Hand Roll Drill except that the football is flipped into the air by the fingers to give it a full back flip, causing the football to come down on the back of the hand. The back of the hand then hits the football upward to give it a full flip forward so it returns to its original position. The quarterback repeats the exercise as many times as he can in 30 seconds.

Coaching Points:

- The quarterback should work both hands equally.

- Once the quarterback becomes adept at the skill with both hands, two footballs can be used at the same time.

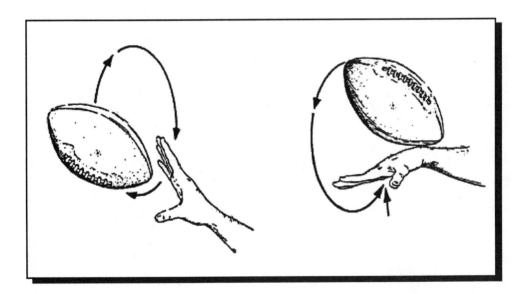

DRILL #85: LATERAL HAND ROLL DRILL

Objective: To develop adept football-handling skills.

Equipment Needed: One or two footballs per quarterback.

Description: The quarterback holds the football by gripping it at one tip with the football facing down perpendicular to the ground. The quarterback then rolls the football laterally over the back of his hand so that he can grab it at its opposite tip. The quarterback then repeats the action in the opposite direction to return it to its original position. The quarterback repeats the exercise as many times as he can execute in 30 seconds.

Coaching Points:

- The quarterback should work both hands equally.
- Once the quarterback becomes adept at the skill with both hands, two footballs can be used at the same time.

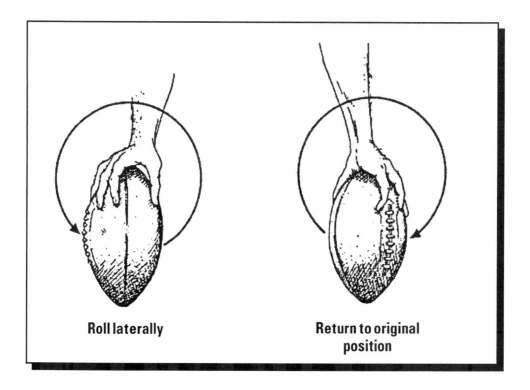

Roll laterally   **Return to original position**

DRILL #86: HAND CIRCLE DRILL

Objective: To develop adept football-handling skills.

Equipment Needed: One or two footballs per quarterback.

Description: The Hand Circle Drill is executed in the same fashion as the Air Dribble Drill except that as the football is dropped, the quarterback circles the football with his hand before he catches it. The quarterback repeats the exercise as many times as he can execute in 30 seconds.

Coaching Points:

- The quarterback should work both hands equally.
- Once the quarterback becomes adept at the skill with both hands, two footballs can be used at the same time.

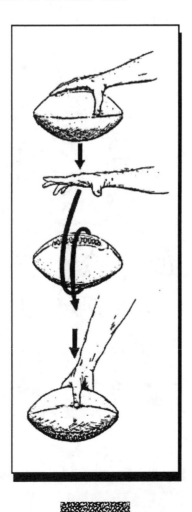

DRILL #87: GLOBETROTTER DRILL

Objective: To develop adept football-handling skills.

Equipment Needed: One football per quarterback.

Description: The quarterback takes a football and passes it from one hand to another behind his back, around his head, over his shoulder, through and around his legs, etc., Globetrotter style. The quarterback should constantly change direction. The quarterback executes the drill for 30 seconds.

Coaching Points:

- Constantly changing direction of the football movement is important.
- The quarterback should be as creative as he can in the combination of Globetrotter-type actions.

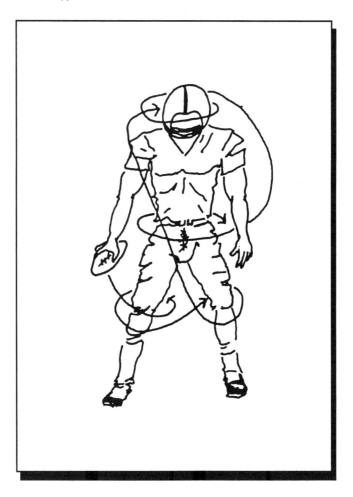

DRILL #88: ONE-HAND JUGGLE DRILL

Objective: To develop adept football-handling skills.

Equipment Needed: Two footballs per quarterback.

Description: The quarterback juggles two footballs at the same time with one hand. The quarterback repeats the exercise for as many repetitions as possible in 30 seconds.

Coaching Points:

• The quarterback should work both hands equally.

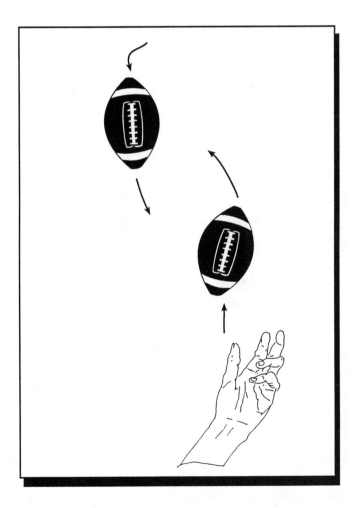

DRILL #89: TWO-HAND JUGGLE DRILL

Objective: To develop adept football-handling skills.

Equipment Needed: Three footballs per quarterback.

Description: The quarterback juggles three footballs at the same time with two hands in a normal juggling fashion. The quarterback repeats the exercise for as many repetitions as possible in 30 seconds.

Coaching Points:

- This exercise is the hardest of the various ball-handling skills drills to execute. The coach may want to allot a full minute to practice the two-football-juggling drill.

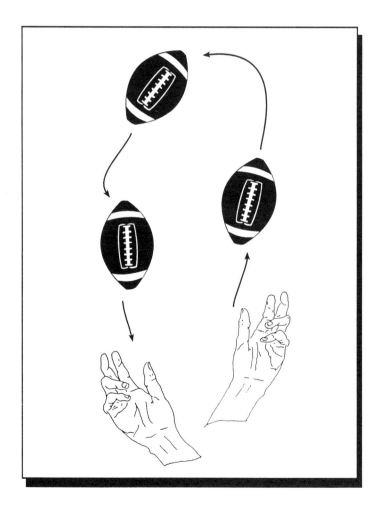

DRILL #90: ONE-HAND FINGER PASSING DRILL

Objective: To develop adept football-handling skills.

Equipment Needed: One football per two quarterbacks.

Description: Two quarterbacks stand apart from one another at a distance of six to seven feet. They toss the football back and forth to one another. All catching and tossing action is done with the fingertips. Each hand should be worked for 30 seconds.

Coaching Points:

- The coach should make sure all catching and tossing is done with the fingertips only.
- The quarterbacks can criss-cross their throws in a figure 8-type fashion to work both hands equally.

DRILL #91: ISO GRIP DRILL

Objective: An isometric exercise to help develop grip strength.

Equipment Needed: One football per quarterback.

Description: The quarterback grips the football with one hand and squeezes it as hard as possible for 10 seconds as an isometric exercise. The quarterback should perform three sets of 10 seconds for each hand.

Coaching Points:

- The quarterback should vary his grip of the football for each repetition, the tip of the football, the fat of the football and in a normal throwing grip position on the laces.

- The quarterback should be sure to exercise both hands, not just his throwing hand.

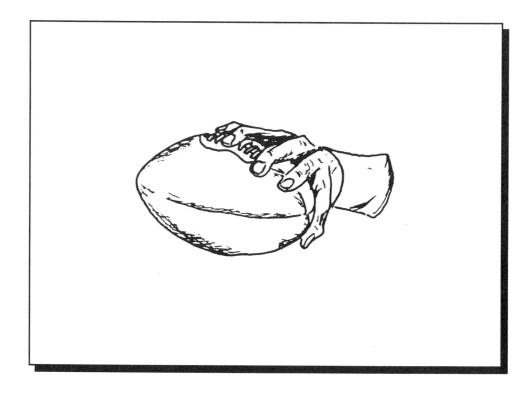

DRILL #92: TWO MAN TUG-O-WAR DRILL

Objective: An isometric type exercise to help develop grip strength.

Equipment Needed: One football per two quarterbacks.

Description: Two quarterbacks each grip the opposite end of the same football. Through steady pressure, they try to pull the ball away from one another in a tug-o-war fashion. They should perform three sets of 10 second for each hand.

Coaching Points:

- The quarterbacks pit right hand grip strength versus right hand grip strength and left versus left to best develop grip strength.

- A quarterback can execute the drill as a one-man isometric drill by gripping both ends of the football, holding the ball in front of the chest and pulling.

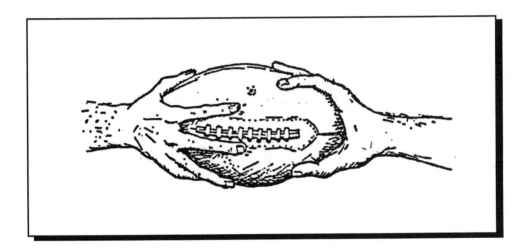

DRILL #93: UNDER ARM BALL ISO DRILL

Objective: An isometric exercise to help develop the vise-like grip and arm strength needed to lock the football away and secure it underneath the armpit.

Equipment Needed: One or two footballs per quarterback.

Description: The quarterback executes a proper one-hand carry of the football and squeezes it into the armpit as hard as he possibly can for 10 seconds as an isometric exercise. He should perform three sets of 10 seconds for each arm.

Coaching Points:

- The quarterbacks should attempt to squeeze the football so hard that they "pop the air out of the ball."

- The coach can quicken the drill by having the quarterback squeeze two footballs, one under each armpit, at the same time.

DRILL #94: PASS HOLD ISO GRIP DRILL

Objective: An isometric exercise to help develop the grip strength a quarterback will need to secure the ball when he is being hit/sacked during a pass attempt.

Equipment Needed: One football per quarterback.

Description: The quarterback assumes a pre-pass delivery stance holding the football in front of the back breast secured with both hands. He then squeezes the football as hard as possible for 10 seconds as an isometric exercise. He should perform three sets of 10 seconds.

Coaching Points:

- The quarterbacks should attempt to squeeze the football so hard that they "pop the air out of the ball."

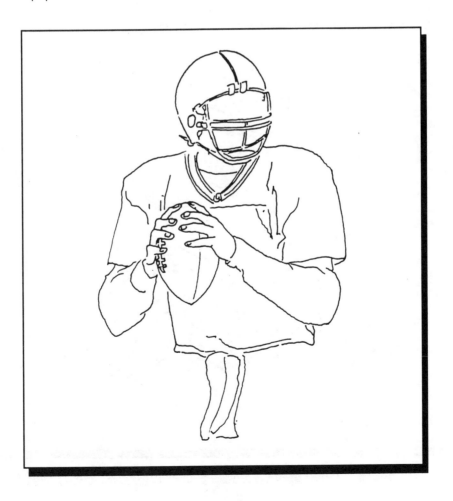

DRILL #95: ARM WRESTLE DRILL

Objective: To practice proper ball-carrying security skills.

Equipment Needed: One football per two quarterbacks.

Description: Two quarterbacks pair up. One executes a proper one-armed carry of the football underneath an armpit. The other quarterback wrestles, grabs, rips, punches, etc., at the football, arm and hand of the quarterback in an attempt to separate the football from the quarterback. The drill is carried out for 30 seconds for each arm for each quarterback.

Coaching Points:

- Extra time can be allotted to the weaker arm and hand of the quarterback.

DRILL #96: GAUNTLET DRILL

Objective: To practice proper ball-carrying security skills.

Equipment Needed: At least two footballs.

Description: One quarterback runs between two lines of quarterbacks (the drill can be done with the running backs to produce sufficient numbers), who slap, rip, punch, etc., at the ball carrying action in attempt to jar the football loose. The two lines should be approximately one and one half yards apart from one another with each quarterback in the line being a yard apart. The quarterback must attempt to run and rip through the gauntlet as fast and as powerfully as possible while executing proper ball carrying security techniques.

Coaching Points:

- The coach should be protective of the quarterback's throwing arm, hand and shoulder. The members of the gauntlet should be kept in check.

- The coach can stand at the mouth of the gauntlet and give the quarterback a simulated defender to make a final cut off of.

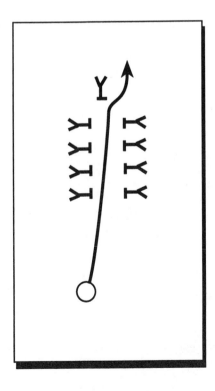

CHAPTER 5

AGILITY/ CONDITIONING DRILLS

DRILL #97: CROSSOVER DROP-STEP AGILITY DRILL

Objective: To develop the quick-foot agility skills needed for the drop-back pass action.

Equipment Needed: One football per quarterback; one flat, low step-over bag or board per quarterback.

Description: The quarterback, with a football in rock carry position, straddles a low, flat step-over bag or board. On command, the quarterback hops in the air and crosses his left leg (for a right-handed quarterback) over the bag in front of him. He then hops and crosses his feet back to their original position. The crossover action is always left foot in front of right foot. The exercise is repeated for two sets of 30 seconds.

Coaching Points:

- Rocking a football across the top of the belly helps to best simulate the normal drop-back action being practiced.

- This drill is a conditioning drill as well as an agility drill. The coach may wish to extend the drill to 60 seconds per set for this exercise.

- The lower the step bag the better. A bevelled board can work just as well. The lower the bag/board, the more natural the crossover action simulating drop-back action.

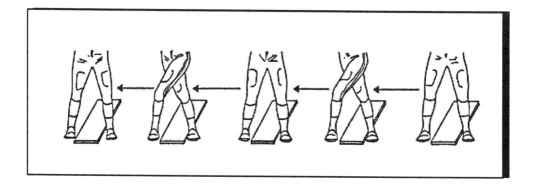

DRILL #98: ROPE CROSSOVER DROP-STEP DRILL

Objective: To develop the quick-foot agility skills needed for the drop-back pass action.

Equipment Needed: One football per quarterback; running rope set.

Description: The quarterback, while rocking a football across his chest, crossover steps (left foot always in front of the right foot for a right-handed quarterback) through a rope course. Once through one side of the rope course, the quarterback turns around and executes the drill coming back the same way. Two sets, down and back in each set, is desirable.

Coaching Points:

- This drill is a bit artificial. The quarterback must prance (knees almost straight up and down) to work the crossover steps through the ropes since he cannot get the desired body tilt that he utilizes in a normal drop. However, the drill does help the quarterback to develop the quick foot agility desired for the drop-back action.

- Rocking a football across the top of the belly helps to best simulate the normal drop-back action being practiced.

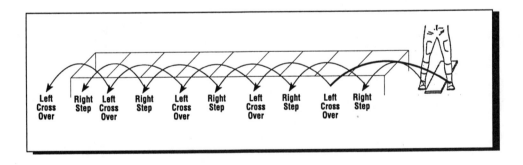

DRILL #99: SKI CONDITIONING DRILL

Objective: To condition the quarterback's legs in a bent knee/squat type position.

Equipment Needed: One football per quarterback; lined field.

Description: The quarterback, gripping a football in his throwing hand, toes the sideline as he straddles a yard line. He then crouches down, bending at the knees as much as possible and not at the hips, in a skier's stance. On the coach's command, the quarterbacks run backwards, remaining in the crouched/knee-bent position, to the hashmarks. They then turn around and repeat the exercise back to the sideline. The drill is repeated for 8-10 repetitions.

Coaching Points:

- Bending at the knees, with the back upright (butt down) is essential.

- Holding/gripping a football helps to simulate drop-back action.

- This drill helps to condition the legs so that the quarterback is bending his legs at the knee joint in his passing stance in the fourth quarter.

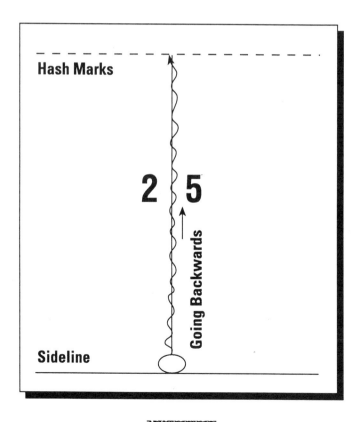

DRILL #100: PASS SET CONDITIONING DRILL

Objective: To specifically condition the quarterbacks by practicing their pass drop set-up.

Equipment Needed: One football per quarterback; lined field.

Description: The quarterbacks all toe the goal line, spaced approximately five yards apart. The coach designates a pass-drop from the offense to execute. One quarterback gives the cadence. All quarterbacks then execute the specific pass drop and pass delivery set-up stance called for by the coach (three-, five-, or seven-step drop, move-out left, move-out right, bootleg left, dive play action right, etc.). After executing the first pass drop set-up, the quarterbacks sprint to realign on the 10 yard line. The pass drops are then repeated all the way down the field for 10 repetitions to the opposite goal line. Up and down the field once is a desired repetition allotment.

Coaching Points:

- The quarterbacks are given a signal (whistle, "go") after each pass drop set up to hustle to the next 10 yard line to reset in a pre-drop, under-the-center stance.

- The coach should check for proper pre-pass delivery stances. As the quarterbacks get tired, they will have a tendency to become lock-legged rather than maintaining proper knee bend. Proper high hold of the football is another area to check as the quarterbacks tire.

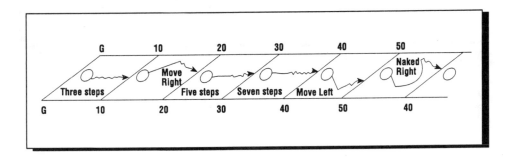

DRILL #101: PASS RE-SET CONDITIONING DRILL

Objective: To specifically condition the quarterbacks by practicing their pass drop sets and resets up and down the field.

Equipment Needed: One football per quarterback; lined field.

Description: The Pass Re-Set Conditioning Drill is executed in the same fashion as the Pass Set Conditioning Drill except that the coach gives three reset commands (step-up, shuffle left/right, bail left/right, duck under) after each set before the quarterback goes to the next 10 yard line.

Coaching Points:

- This drill is taxing physically. One set of 10 repetitions is usually sufficient.

- As the quarterbacks tire, the coach should be sure to check for proper knee bend and high hold of the football.

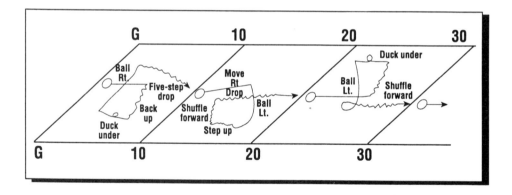

Steve Axman is the head football coach at Northern Arizona University. In his eight seasons at the helm of the NAU football program, Axman has led the Lumberjacks to national prominence. The 1996 season was highlighted by NAU's first-ever appearance in the Division I-AA postseason tournament. In addition, NAU became the first college team—at any level—to have both a 2,000-yard rusher (1996 Walter Payton Award winner Archie Amerson) and a 3,000-yard passer (Travis Brown) in a single season.

Prior to assuming his present position in 1990, Axman was on the coaching staff at the University of Maryland, where he coached the quarterbacks—most notably New York Jets signal caller Neil O'Donnell. Before his stint in Maryland, Axman served as the offensive coordinator at UCLA from 1987 to 1988. During his tenure on the Bruins' staff, Axman coached the quarterbacks—one of whom was NFL great Troy Aikman of the Dallas Cowboys. Axman has also coached pro quarterbacks Jeff Lewis (Denver Broncos) and Scott Zolak (New England Patriots). A 1969 graduate of C.W. Post College, Axman has also held positions on the gridiron staffs of Stanford University, the Denver Gold (USFL), the University of Arizona, the University of Illinois, the U.S. Military Academy, Albany State University, and East Stroudsburg State University.

A 29-year coaching veteran, Axman is widely renowned as having one of the most creative offensive minds in the game. An accomplished writer, he has authored several books and articles on football schemes, techniques and strategies, including the well received *Coaching Offensive Backs* (1998). Axman has also produced three highly successful instructional videos: *Coaching Offensive Backs*; *Winning Quarterback Drills*; and *Coaching Quarterback Passing Mechanics*.

Axman and his wife, Dr. Marie Axman, reside in Flagstaff, Arizona. They have four daughters—Mary Beth, Jaclyn, Melissa, and Kimberly.

ADDITIONAL FOOTBALL RESOURCES FROM

COACHES CHOICE

BOOKS:

■ *COACHING QUARTERBACK PASSING MECHANICS*
by Steve Axman
1998 ▪ Paper ▪ 80 pp
ISBN 1-57167-194-3 ▪ $16.95

■ *COACHING OFFENSIVE BACKS (2nd Ed.)*
by Steve Axman
1997 ▪ Paper ▪ 216 pp
ISBN 1-57167-088-2 ▪ $19.95

VIDEOS:

■ *COACHING OFFENSIVE BACKS*
by Steve Axman
1997 ▪ Running Time: Approx. 48 min.
ISBN 1-57167-119-6 ▪ $40.00

■ *COACHING QUARTERBACK PASSING MECHANICS*
by Steve Axman
1998 ▪ Running Time: Approx. 41 min.
ISBN 1-57167-225-7 ▪ $40.00

■ *WINNING QUARTERBACK DRILLS*
by Steve Axman
1998 ▪ Running Time: Approx. 40 min.
ISBN 1-57167-226-5 ▪ $40.00

TO PLACE YOUR ORDER:

REEDSWAIN
BOOKS & VIDEOS
FREE CATALOG CALL
1-800-331-5191

COACHES CHOICE B_____ n, IL 61824-0647,